Daily Math
Warm-Ups
Grade Four

by
M.J. Owen

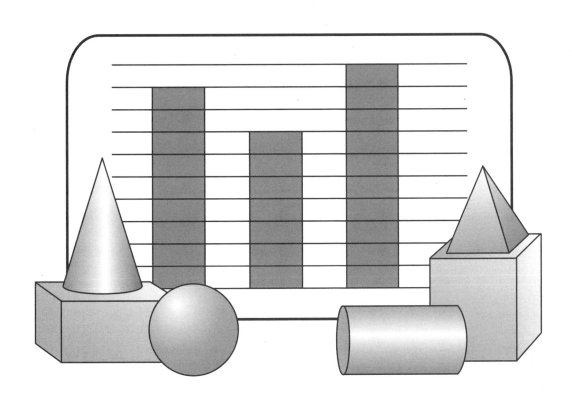

Carson-Dellosa Publishing Company, Inc.
Greensboro, North Carolina

Credits

Editors
Hank Rudisill
Sabena Maiden

Cover Design
Dez Perrotti

Cover Photo
EyeWire Images

Layout Design
Hank Rudisill

Art Coordinator
Betsy Peninger

Artists
Jon Nawrocik
Julie Kinlaw

Printed in the USA • All rights reserved   ISBN 0-88724-820-9

Table of Contents
Daily Math Warm-Ups Grade Four

Introduction to *Daily Math Warm-Ups*

Based on standards specified by the National Council of Teachers of Mathematics (NCTM), *Daily Math Warm-Ups* will give teachers a year-long collection of challenging problems that reinforce math skills taught in the classroom. Designed around the traditional school year, the series offers 180 daily lessons (sets of five problems each) including computation, graph, and word problems. For each two-week group of lessons, an eight-problem multiple-choice assessment is provided to help you easily identify which students have mastered which concepts. The daily practice will help improve students' skills and bolster their confidence.

How to Use This Book

You can use this book in the following ways:
- Use the problems as a daily math warm-up. Make each child responsible for keeping a math journal which is checked periodically. Copy the daily lessons on transparencies. At the beginning of each class, put the problems on an overhead and give students approximately five minutes to solve the problems. When students have completed the exercise, go over the problems as a class. You can use this opportunity to discuss why some answers are correct and others are not.
- Because copying from the board or overhead is challenging for some learners, you may choose to photocopy the daily lessons for particular students, or for the entire class. Have students work on the problems at the beginning of class, then continue as described above.
- Give each student a copy of the problems near the end of class and have them turn the work in as a "Ticket Out the Door." You can then check students' work and then return their work and go over the answers at the beginning of the next class period.

Daily Math Warm-Ups includes many elements that will help students master a wide range of mathematical concepts. These include:

- 180 five-problem lessons based on standards specified by the National Council of Teachers of Mathematics

- 18 multiple-choice assessment tests in standardized-test format, to help identify concepts mastered and concepts in need of reteaching

- 12 real-world application extension activities

- A reproducible problem-solving strategy guide for students (on the inside back cover)

- Plenty of computation, graph, and word-problem solving opportunities that become more difficult as students progress through the school year

Lesson 1

1. $708 - 59 =$

2. $2{,}123 + 3{,}456 =$

3. On the line below, write the word form of the ordinal number. 21st

   _____

4. Sarah and Frankie were playing video games. Sarah scored 21,456 points, and Frankie scored 9,087 points. How many points did Sarah and Frankie score altogether?

   Sarah and Frankie scored _____ points altogether.

5. Write the number in standard form.
   one hundred thousand, eighty-seven

   _____

Lesson 2

1. Write the number in standard form.
   $60{,}000 + 5{,}000 + 300 + 3$ _____

2. $19{,}007 - 12{,}456 =$

3. $33{,}876 + 29{,}008 =$

4. Write the number in expanded form.
   fifty-nine thousand, six

   _____

5. A fund-raiser for The Children's Museum raised $44,609. The museum spent $9,081 on food and beverages. How much money did the museum make after paying for food and beverages?

   The museum made _____ after paying for food and beverages.

Lesson 3

1. $13.58 + $76.49 =

2.   Put the numbers in order from least to greatest.
     7,567   17,456   7,656   71,555   7,444

     _____

3.   Write the number in standard form.
     200,000,000 + 7,000,000 + 600,000 + 30,000 + 2,000 + 700 + 70

     _____

4.   Dana has to pay $10,990 for her college dorm room and tuition each
     year. How much money does Dana spend the first 2 years of college?

     Dana spends a total _____ the first 2 years she is in college.

5.   Write the number six million, four hundred thousand, two.

     _____

Lesson 4

1.   Round 54,878 to the nearest ten thousand.

     _____

2.   49,007 – 34,569 =

3.   45,678 + 21,456 =

4.   Louis takes $100.75 on vacation. He spends $16.75 on souvenirs,
     $27.55 on food, and $44.50 on train fare. How much money does
     Louis have left?

     Louis has _____ left.

5.   Round 43,766 to the nearest thousand. _____

Lesson 5

1. Fill in the blank with <, >, or = to make the number sentence true.

   17,987 _____ 17,877

2. Write the number in standard form.
   twelve million, six hundred thousand, eight

   _____

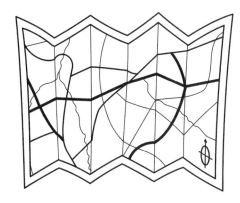

3. 7 x 12 =

4. 6 x 62 =

5. Chelsea's family traveled 300 miles by car each day during their family vacation. How many miles did Chelsea's family travel over all 6 days?

   Chelsea's family traveled a total of _____ miles.

Lesson 6

1. Rachel filled all 15 shelves in her room with books. She placed 9 books on each shelf. How many books did she place on all 15 shelves?

   Rachel placed _____ books total on all 15 shelves.

2. 76 x 8 =

3. 35 ÷ 7 =

4. Write the number three million, four hundred ninety-six thousand, seven hundred seventy-two in expanded form.

   _____

5. Put the numbers in order from greatest to least.
   54,657   55,678   45,656   54,607   54,922

   _____

Lesson 7

1. Fill in the blank with <, >, or = to make the number sentence true.

   37,700 _____ 37,607

2. 81 x 9 =

3. 68 ÷ 2 =

4. $898.70 – $876.58 =

5. A moving company is able to move 92 boxes every hour. How many boxes are they able to move during an 8-hour workday?

   They are able to move _____ boxes during an 8-hour workday.

Lesson 8

1. Put the numbers in order from greatest to least.
   $99.09 $99.87 $90.87 $99.90 $99.99

   _____

2. What is the value of the 5 in the number 4,567,433?

   _____

3. 84 ÷ 4 =

4. Ellie has 150 CDs. She wants to store an equal number of her CDs in 2 containers. How many CDs should Ellie put in each container?

   Ellie should put _____ CDs in each container.

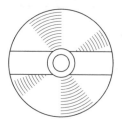

5. Write the number in standard form.
   one hundred forty million, six hundred eighty-seven

   _____

Lesson 9

1. $56,789 - 34,577 =$

2. Write the numbers in order from least to greatest.
   $76.67 $77.89 $77.76 $76.77 $77.06

   _____

3. Write the number in expanded form.
   nine million, three hundred thirty-nine thousand, six

   _____

4. Which number is in the millions place?
   45,432,333 _____

5. The art teacher has a bowl containing 99 beads. A group of 11 friends in the class decide to make bracelets. They plan to divide the beads evenly. How many beads will each friend get?

   Each friend will get _____ beads.

Lesson 10

1. Write the number in standard form.
   $8,000,000 + 900,000 + 4,000 + 500 + 3$

   _____

2. $27 \times 8 =$

3. $41 \times 6 =$

4. 32 boys are traveling by bus to camp. There are 4 buses headed to the camp. If the same number of boys are on each bus, how many boys are on each bus?

   There are _____ boys on each bus.

5. $7,678.55 + $5,444.50 =$

Lesson 11

1. $64 \div y = 8$ $y =$ _____

2. Julie has 17 dimes in her pocket. What is the total value of the money that Julie is carrying?

   The total value of the money that Julie is carrying is _____.

Fill in the missing number to make each number sentence true.

3. $7,067 - y = 4,002$ $y =$ _____

4. $16,545 + y = 24,345$ $y =$ _____

5. Write the multiplication number sentence that the picture shows. Then, solve the problem.

   _____

   _____

Lesson 12

1. Fill in the blank with <, >, or = to make the number sentence true.
   54,657 _____ 54,989

2. There are 82 trees at a park. Half of the trees are pecan trees and the other half are oak trees. How many trees at the park are oak trees?

   _____ trees are oak trees.

3. $78 \div 6 =$

4. $65 \div y = 13$ $y =$ _____

5. $34,786 - y = 23,119$ $y =$ _____

Lesson 13

1. Megan goes to the movies 19 times during the summer. Every time she goes to the movies, she spends $9 on a ticket and $8 on soda and popcorn. How much money does Megan spend on movie admission and refreshments during the summer?

   Megan spends a total of _____ on a ticket and refreshments.

2. Fill in the blank with <, >, or = to make the number sentence true.
   121,453 _____ 112,678

3. 48 x 9 =

4. 115 ÷ 5 =

5. In the box, draw squares to represent the number sentence 42 ÷ 6 = .

Lesson 14

1. On Saturday, 234,543 people traveled through the Hardy International Airport. On Sunday, 344,456 people traveled through the same airport. What is the total number of people who traveled through the airport on Saturday and Sunday combined?

   _____ people traveled through the airport on Saturday and Sunday combined.

2. Fill in the blank with <, >, or = to make the number sentence true.
   786,454 _____ 786,454

3. Fill in the blank with the missing number in the series.
   820, 850, _____, 910, 940, 970

4. 59 x 8 =

5. 880 ÷ 2 =

Lesson 15

1. Last year, Langdon School had $127,657 available for scholarships. This year, Langdon School has $141,509 available. How much more money does the school have for scholarships this year?

   Langdon has _____ more this year.

2. 89 x 4 =

3. 67 x 8 =

4. 212 ÷ 4 =

5. Draw a picture in the box to represent the number sentence 12 x 4.

Lesson 16

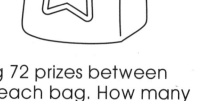

1. y x 6 = 54   y = _____

2. 543,786 + 89,009 =

3. 120 ÷ 10 =

4. Fill in the blanks to complete the pattern.
   Z, Y, A, B, X, W, C, D, _____, _____, E, F

5. For the school carnival, the principal is dividing 72 prizes between 9 bags. She puts an equal number of prizes in each bag. How many prizes does she put in each bag?

   She puts _____ prizes in each bag.

Lesson 17

1. $10 \div 10 =$

2. $12 \times 9 =$

3. $78{,}908 - y = 40{,}000$ $y =$ _____

4. Ella earned $435.05 during the month of June and $543.75 during the month of July. How much money did Ella earn during June and July?

    Ella earned _____ during June and July.

5. Fill in the blank with <, >, or = to make the number sentence true.

    $87{,}877$ _____ $877{,}505$

Lesson 18

1. Javier is writing a book report. The total length of his book report is 120 pages. He writes an equal number of pages during 12 days. How many pages does Javier write each day?

    Javier writes _____ pages each day.

2. $70 \times 7 =$

3. $70 \div 7 =$

4. $14{,}543 - 13{,}999 =$

5. Look at the picture. On the lines below, write 2 number sentences that the picture could represent. Then, solve the problems.

_____

_____

Lesson 19

1. 65 x 9 =

2. 250 ÷ 5 =

3. 87,602 − 59,899 =

4. Exactly 56,959 people attended a basketball playoff game on Wednesday night. Of those, 36,518 fans wore red jerseys. On Thursday night, 77,401 people attend a playoff game. How many more people attended the game on Thursday than on Wednesday?

   _____ more people attended the game on Thursday.

5. Look at the pattern. Fill in the missing even numbers.
   200, 400, 800, _____, _____, 6,400, _____

Lesson 20

1. 50 x 1 =

2. y − 43,987 = 78,644   y = _____

3. 6 x 9 =

4. Jay mows one lawn every day Monday through Saturday. He is paid $25 for each lawn that he mows. How much money does Jay earn mowing lawns Monday through Saturday?

   Jay earns a total of _____ mowing lawns Monday through Saturday.

5. Draw the missing angles in the pattern below.

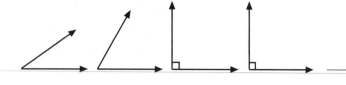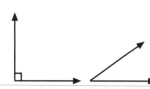

Lesson 21

1. A total of 100 fourth graders are being divided equally between 5 fourth-grade teachers. How many students will be in each class?

    There will be _____ fourth-grade students in each class.

2. Round each number to the nearest thousand.
    16,567 _____   1,265 _____   37,890 _____

3. $y - 31,876 = 97,808$ $y =$ _____

4. $14,543 + y = 41,208$ $y =$ _____

5. Look at the bar graph. How many more people subscribed in September than August?

    _____ more people subscribed in September than August.

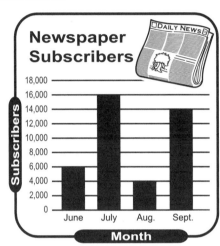

Lesson 22

1. Macy eats 33 animal crackers as a snack every day after school. How many animal crackers does she eat during a 5-day school week?

    Macy eats _____ animal crackers during a 5-day school week.

2. $y - 12,876 = 18,999$ $y =$ _____

3. $38 \times 6 =$

4. $(567 + 89) - 17 =$

5. Look at the bar graph. How many more people watched "Dinosaurs" and "Love & Money" than "Bob & Becky" and "Ricky?"

    _____ more people watched "Dinosaurs" and "Love & Money."

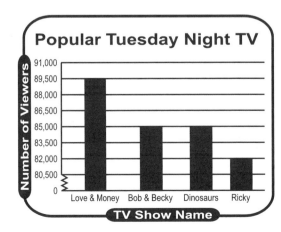

Lesson 23

1. Round each number to the nearest ten thousand.
    56,765 _____   123,098 _____   71,003 _____

2. There are 10 signs for each 2 miles of highway. How many signs are on 24 miles of highway?

    There are _____ signs on 24 miles of highway.

3. $52 \times 9 =$

4. $16,455 - 12,999 =$

5. Look at the graph. How many E-mails did Ida receive on Tuesday, Thursday, and Saturday combined?

    Ida received _____ E-mails on Tuesday, Thursday, and Saturday combined.

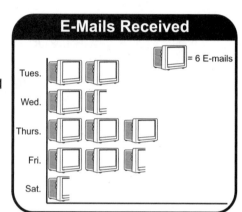

Lesson 24

1. The town hall's bells ring 8 times every hour. How many times do the bells chime in a 24-hour period?

    The bells chime _____ times in a 24 hour period.

2. $37 \times 3 =$

3. $56 \div 4 =$

4. $(166 - 7) + 212 =$

5. The bar graph shows the number of students enrolled at 5 elementary schools. Put the schools' names in order from greatest to least enrollment.

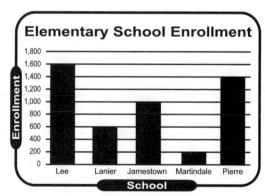

Lesson 25

1. Delicia needs to read 34 pages of her book each day on Friday, Saturday, and Sunday nights so she will be finished in time for her test on Monday. How many pages total does Delicia need to read on Friday, Saturday, and Sunday nights?

   Delicia needs to read a total of _____ pages on Friday, Saturday, and Sunday nights.

2. $100 \times 4 =$

3. $90 \div 9 =$

4. $66 \times 5 =$

5. The pictograph shows the number of passengers who traveled on the airport shuttle bus each day. How many more passengers traveled on the shuttle bus on Wednesday and Thursday than on Monday and Tuesday?

   _____ more people traveled on the shuttle bus on Wednesday and Thursday.

Airport Shuttle Passengers

= 70 passengers

Mon.
Tues.
Wed.
Thurs.

Lesson 26

1. $(197 - 19) + 21 =$

2. $10 \times 10 =$

3. $72 \div 8 =$

4. Round each number to the nearest thousand.
   15,454 _____   2,345 _____   89,098 _____

5. Betsy practices 64 multiplication facts each day. How many facts does she practice in 3 days?

   Betsy practices a total of _____ multiplication facts in 3 days.

Name _____

Lesson 27

1. The baseball coach needs to divide 180 balls equally between 3 teams. How many balls should the baseball coach give to each team?

    The baseball coach should give _____ balls to each team.

2. 121,456 + 76,411 =

3. 41 x 9 =

4. 47,567 – y = 14,655
    y = _____

5. Based on the information provided in the pictograph, if twice as many fourth graders wore green shirts than blue shirts, how many fourth graders wore green shirts on field day?

    _____ students wore green shirts on field day.

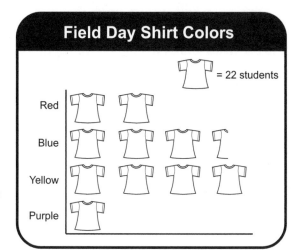

Field Day Shirt Colors

= 22 students

Red
Blue
Yellow
Purple

Lesson 28

1. 6 friends pick apples together in September. They pick a total of 96 apples. They want to divide the apples equally among themselves. How many apples should each friend get?

    Each friend should get _____ apples.

2. 28 x 7 =

3. 49 ÷ 7 =

4. (338 – 179) + 18 =

5. Look at the table. How many more minutes did Caroline spend running and jumping rope than lifting weights and playing tag?

    Caroline spent _____ more minutes running and jumping rope.

Time Spent Exercising

Exercise	Minutes
Running	122
Playing Tag	68
Jumping Rope	29
Lifting Weights	49
Swimming	33

Lesson 29

1. A letter carrier sorts 17,500 pieces of mail on Friday and 9,876 pieces of mail on Saturday. How many more pieces of mail did the letter carrier sort on Friday than on Saturday?

    The letter carrier sorted _____ more pieces of mail on Friday than on Saturday.

2. $60 \div 5 =$

3. $28 \div 4 =$

4. $38 \times 2 =$

5. Look at the bar graph. If Matt's brother, Ken, took half as many pictures as Matt, how many pictures did Ken take?

    Ken took _____ pictures.

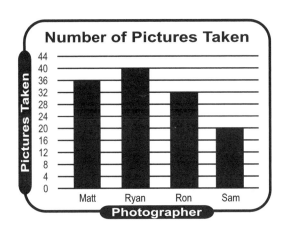

Lesson 30

1. Jermaine plants 45 flowers. He plants an equal number of flowers in each of 5 rows. How many flowers does Jermaine plant in each row?

    Jermaine plants _____ flowers in each row.

2. Based on the pictograph, which of the following statements is true?
    A. The 5th graders read 24 books during the summer.
    B. 4th graders read twice as many books as 2nd graders.
    C. 3rd graders read twice as many books as 2nd graders.

3. $34,567 - 12,453 =$

4. $24 \times 9 =$

5. $(52 + 67 + 12) - 15 =$

Daily Math Warm-Ups Grade 4

Lesson 31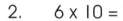

1. Mr. Simpson made a pie graph with his students. It showed the amounts of time they spent on different subjects during their 8-hour school day. How many hours each day do Mr. Simpson's students spend on reading and math combined?

   They spend _____ hours on reading and math combined.

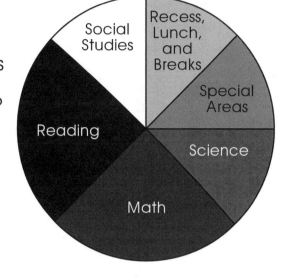

2. 6 x 10 =

3. 7 x 20 =

4. 14 x 9 =

5. On the line, write the number four million, seven hundred sixty-nine.

Lesson 32

1. Madeline spends 4 hours at the gym each week. How much time does she spend at the gym during an 8 week, or 2 month, period?

   Madeline spends a total of _____ hours at the gym during two months.

2. The table shows the prices of school supplies at the school store. Melissa bought 3 pencils and 3 erasers. How much money did she spend in all?

   Melissa spent _____ in all.

School Store Supplies	
Item	**Price**
Pencil	5 for $.25
Notebook	$2.00 each
Eraser	1 for $.50 or 2 for $.75
Crayons	$1.25 each
Poster Board	$.55 each

3. 32,323 + 567 =

4. 9 x 9 =

5. 6,567 – 3,454 =

Lesson 33

1. Mandy has 48 necklaces in a large jar. She has an equal number of green, blue, red, and purple necklaces. How many green necklaces does Mandy have?

    Mandy has _____ green necklaces.

2. Using the information from the pictograph, circle the number sentence that should be used to determine the total number of lunches sold on Wednesday, Thursday, and Friday.
    A.   400 + 500 + 450 =
    B.   400 + 250 + 350 =
    C.   350 + 425 + 225 =
    D.   400 + 500 + 350 =

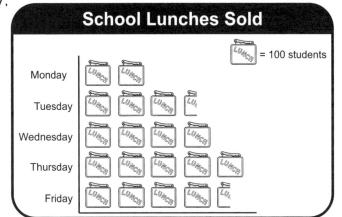

3. 12 x 2 =

4. 40 x 9 =

5. 11 x 11 =

Lesson 34

1. Jarrod isn't sure what time he needs to get up for school. He knows it will take him 30 minutes to shower and get dressed, 30 minutes to eat breakfast and wash his dishes, and 15 minutes to ride the bus to school. If school starts at 9 A.M., what time does Jarrod need to get up?

    Jarrod needs to get up at _____ .

2. 42 x 2 =

3. 15 x 5 =

4. 43,001 – 29,075 =

5. Look at the table. How much more money did Leslie spend on ice cream and milk than on grapes?

Leslie's Trip to the Store		
Item	Quantity	Price
Grapes	2 pounds	$2.00 per pound
Milk	1 gallon	$2.75 per gallon
Newspaper	1 paper	$.50 each
Ice Cream	1 pint	$3.50 per pint

    Leslie spent _____ more on ice cream and milk than on grapes.

Lesson 35

1. Round the answer to the nearest ten thousands place.
   43,878 + 21,989 =

2. 22 x 8 =

3. 49 x 9 =

4. 30 x 4 =

5. Based on the information in the table, how many magazines will be sold during Week 5?

   _____ magazines will be sold during Week 5.

Magazines Sold	
Week	Units Sold
1	10
2	35
3	60
4	85
5	

Lesson 36

1. Sarah had $20.00. On Saturday night, she spent $10.00 on dinner, $5.75 on a movie, and $2.50 on popcorn and soda. How much money does Sarah have left?

   Sarah has _____ left.

2. 40 ÷ 4 =

3. 18 ÷ 2 =

4. 36 ÷ 6 =

5. Look at the bar graph. How many more people like romantic and action movies better than mystery and comedy movies?

   _____ people like romantic and action movies better than mystery and comedy movies.

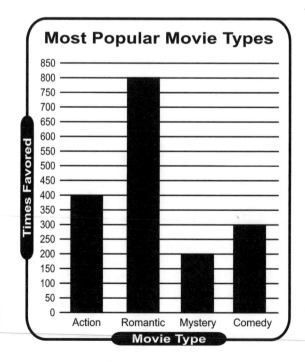

Lesson 37

1. Danny is shopping for gifts for his mother and sister. He buys a picture frame for his mother. The picture frame costs $10. He buys a bag of candy for his sister. The bag of candy costs $2. Danny pays with one $10 bill and one $5 bill. How much change will Danny receive?

   Danny will receive _____ change.

2. $42 \div 2 =$

3. $90 \div 6 =$

4. $15 \div 5 =$

5. Half of the total number of people who voted for their favorite pets are girls, and the other half are boys. Based on the information provided in the graph, how many boys voted for their favorite pets?

   _____ boys voted for their favorite pets.

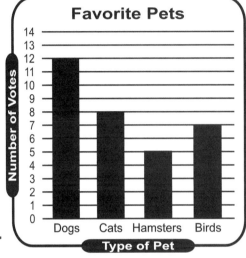

Lesson 38

1. On a busy Friday night, a pizza restaurant sold 54 pizzas. On Saturday, they sold 3 times as many pizzas. How many pizzas did they sell on Saturday?

   They sold _____ pizzas on Saturday.

2. $14,567 - 12,994 =$

3. $75 \div 5 =$

4. $25 \times 4 =$

5. Based on the pattern in the table, how many cars were parked on Avenue C on Friday?

   _____ cars were parked on Avenue C on Friday.

Cars Parked on Avenue C	
Day	Number of Cars
Monday	12
Tuesday	24
Wednesday	48
Thursday	96

Lesson 39

1. There are 365 days during the year. If 211 days are sunny, 97 days are rainy, and the remaining days are snowy, how many days are snowy?

    _____ days are snowy.

2. $110 \div 10 =$

3. $85 \times 9 =$

4. $91 \times 8 =$

5. Molly's mom is helping Molly save money for a new bike. She tells Molly she will match the amount of money that Molly is able to earn during June, July, August, and September combined. How much money should Molly's mom add to Molly's account?

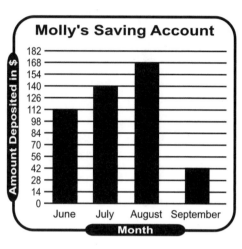

    Molly's mom should add _____ into Molly's account.

Lesson 40

1. A group of 8 buses is taking students on a field trip. The buses will travel 16 miles to the art museum. There are 59 students on each bus. How many students are on all 8 buses?

    There are _____ students on all 8 buses.

2. $18 \times 9 =$

3. $54 \div 6 =$

4. $71 \times 8 =$

5. Half as many people like cream pie more than blueberry pie. How many people like cream pie best? Fill in your answer on the bar graph and on the line below.

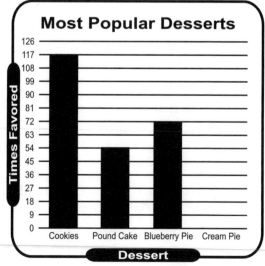

    _____ people like cream pie best.

Lesson 41

1. At Brook Hollow Elementary School, there are 228 students in the third, fourth, fifth, and sixth grades combined. There are an equal number of students in each grade. How many students are in each grade?

   There are _____ students in each grade.

2. 9 x 8 =

3. 150 x 4 =

4. 39 x 7 =

5. Look at the octagon. How many vertices does an octagon have?

   _____

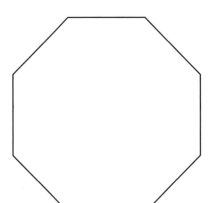

Lesson 42

1. 56,234 – 29,981 =

2. Fill in the blanks to complete the pattern.
   4, 16, _____, 256, _____, 4,096

3. Audrey's class earns $612 selling candy bars during the first semester of the school year. Each candy bar they sell costs $3. How many candy bars did Audrey's class sell?

   Audrey's class sold _____ candy bars.

4. 302 x 8 =

5. 14 x 6 =

Lesson 43

1. 124 x 6 =

2. 7 x 6 =

3. 251 x 8 =

4. Is the line on the picture of the house a line of symmetry? Why or why not?

   _____

   _____

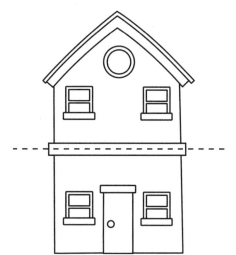

5. Look at the table. What fraction of the cars sold during May were red? _____

Number of Cars Sold in May					
Color	Red	Blue	Silver	Green	White	Black
Amount	8	9	15	4	3	16

Lesson 44

1. 340 ÷ 4 =

2. Joey has 15 jars of marbles in his room. He has 338 marbles in each jar. Joey plans to give away 517 of his marbles this weekend. How many marbles does Joey have in all 15 jars of marbles now?

   Joey has _____ marbles now.

3. 287 x 1 =

4. 433 x 9 =

5. Look at the 4 shapes. On each line, write "yes" if each shape is a polygon.

Lesson 45

1. One of these shapes is not a quadrilateral. Write "yes" or "no" if each is a quadrilateral. Then, on the lines below, explain why one is not a quadrilateral.

    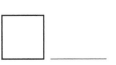 

    _____

    _____

2. $378 \div 3 =$

3. $551 \times 9 =$

4. $6 \times 4 =$

5. Write the missing letter to complete the pattern. Z A V E R _____ N

Lesson 46

1. A sold-out concert is playing at Sunset Gardens on Friday, Saturday, and Sunday nights. 779 tickets have been sold for each night of the performance. How many tickets were sold for all 3 nights total?

    _____ tickets were sold for all 3 nights total.

2. $987 \times 9 =$

3. How many vertices do 3 hexagons have? _____

4. Tim and Lynn each baked a chocolate pie. Tim ate $\frac{2}{6}$ of his pie and Lynn ate $\frac{1}{3}$ of her pie.
    Which of the following statements is true?
    A.   Tim ate more chocolate pie.
    B.   Lynn ate more chocolate pie.
    C.   Tim and Lynn ate the same amount of chocolate pie.

5. $815 \div 5 =$

27

Lesson 47

1. Draw an angle in the blank to complete the pattern.

2. $56,019 - 48,998 =$

3. $809 \times 2 =$

4. $48 \div 6 =$

5. Look at the fraction in the box. Fill in the circle so that an equivalent fraction is shown.

$$\frac{4}{5}$$

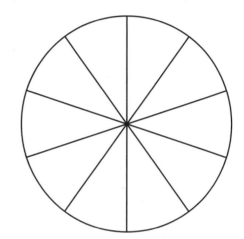

Lesson 48

1. Circle the statement that best describes what is happening in the pattern. 59, 57, 62, 60, 65, 63, 68, 66, 71
   A. First, 2 is being added. Then, 5 is being subtracted.
   B. First, 2 is being subtracted. Then, 5 is being added.
   C. First, 3 is being subtracted. Then, 4 is being added.
   D. First, 1 is being subtracted. Then, 5 is being added.

2. $38 \div 2 =$

3. $318 \times 7 =$

4. $543 \times 6 =$

5. Jesse is 7 and Lee is 11. Jesse has saved $51. If Lee has saved 5 times as much money as Jesse, how much money has Lee saved?

   Lee has saved _____.

Name _____

Lesson 49

1. Estimate the answer to the nearest hundred thousands place.
   786,766 + 232,980 =

2. Marie is waiting in line to get tickets for a play. Including Marie, there are 1,001 people in line. There are 56 people in front of Marie. How many people are behind Marie?

   _____ people are behind Marie in line.

3. 77 x 7 =

4. 72 ÷ 6 =

5. Determine the pattern in the table. Fill in the missing numbers under the heading "Grocery Bill."

Grocery Store Spending

Month	Grocery Bill
January	
February	$45
March	$85
April	$55
May	$95
June	$65
July	
August	

Lesson 50

1. José is training for a marathon. He runs 34 miles the first week and 29 miles the next week. During his third week of training, he wants to run as many miles as he ran the first 2 weeks combined. He plans to run an equal number of miles during each of the 7 days of the week. How many miles will José run each day?

   José will run _____ miles each day.

2. Round each number in the problem to the nearest ten thousand. Then, solve the problem.
   76,980 − 34,767 =

3. 675 ÷ 5 =

4. 908 x 7 =

5. Circle the fraction that is equivalent to $\frac{3}{4}$.
   $\frac{3}{5}$ $\frac{9}{12}$ $\frac{10}{15}$ $\frac{1}{3}$

Lesson 51

1. $\dfrac{2}{3} = \dfrac{y}{12}$ y = _____

2. Circle the number sentence that should be used to solve the problem. Perry is planning to mail 800 letters. He has put stamps on $\dfrac{3}{4}$ of the letters. How many letters does Perry still need to stamp?

   A. $800 \div 2 =$ B. $800 \div 4 =$

   C. $800 + 4 =$ D. $800 \times 4 =$

3. $1.2 \times 7 =$

4. $60 \times 66 =$

5. Look at the grid and the location key. Which place is located at the coordinate (4,3) on the map?
   A.   Pete's Pizza
   B.   Betty's Beauty Shop
   C.   Ben's Bowling Alley
   D.   Izzy's Ice Cream Shop

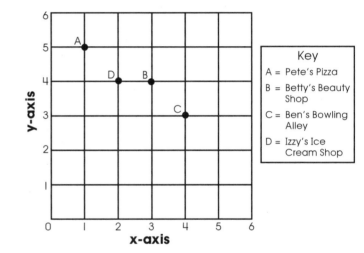

Key
A = Pete's Pizza
B = Betty's Beauty Shop
C = Ben's Bowling Alley
D = Izzy's Ice Cream Shop

Lesson 52

1. Fill in the blank with <, >, or = to make the number sentence true.
   123,565 _____ 103,564

2. $\dfrac{4}{y} = \dfrac{1}{3}$ y = _____

3. $6.2 \times 70 =$

4. $90 \div 5 =$

5. Look at the following pattern, or net. If you cut out and folded the net, what 3-dimensional figure would you have?

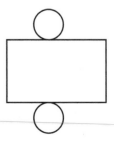

_____

Lesson 53

1. Peter attends 6 dance lessons each week, all year long. There are 52 weeks in a year. Peter missed 5 dance lessons while sick. How many dance lessons did Peter attend during the year?

   Peter attended _____ dance lessons during the year.

2. $504 \div 4 =$

3. $78 \times 9 =$

4. $678 \times 4 =$

5. Add a point to the grid at each of the following 4 coordinates. Label the points.
   A. (2,1)
   B. (4,5)
   C. (1,2)
   D. (4,4)

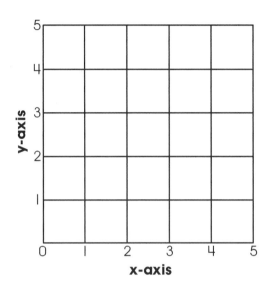

Lesson 54

1. $0.75 \times 6 =$

2. $\frac{7}{8} = \frac{y}{56}$ $y =$ _____

3. $788 \times 9 =$

4. $280 \div 4 =$

5. Look at the following pattern, or net. If you cut out and folded the net, what 3-dimensional figure would you have?

   _____

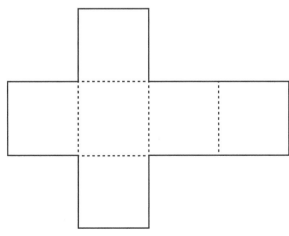

Lesson 55

1. On which coordinate is the heart located?
   A. (8,6)
   B. (3,2)
   C. (4,1)
   D. (6,8)

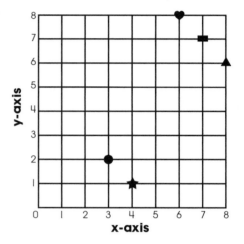

2. $900 \div 9 =$

3. $89.4 \times 9 =$

4. $987 \times 45 =$

5. Fill in the blank with <, >, or = to make the number sentence true.
   76,876 _____ 76,768

Lesson 56

1. $\dfrac{1}{8} = \dfrac{3}{y}$ $y =$ _____

2. $67,987 - 32,998 =$

3. $811 \times 50 =$

4. If each side of a cube is valued at $1.25, what is the total value of the entire cube?

   _____

5. Annabelle is setting up chairs for a school play. She sets up 59 rows of seats. She places 16 seats in each row. How many seats does Annabelle set up for the school play?

   Annabelle set up _____ seats for the school play.

Lesson 57

1. Look at the following pattern, or net. If you cut out and fold the net, what 3-dimensional figure will you have?

_____

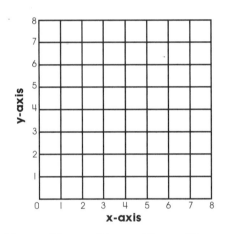

3. 298 x 60 =

4. 456 ÷ 6 =

2. Lisa has 288 blocks. If $\frac{1}{2}$ of the blocks are yellow and the rest of the blocks are orange, how many of Lisa's blocks are orange?

_____ of Lisa's blocks are orange.

5. Add a point to the grid at each of the following 4 coordinates. Label the points.
   A. (5,6)
   B. (3,4)
   C. (2,7)
   D. (1,8)

Lesson 58

1. 22.7 x 6 =

2. 654 x 80 =

3. $\frac{1}{3} = \frac{6}{y}$ y = _____

4. Wesley has $10 in his pocket. When he goes to dinner, he orders a hamburger and fries for $4.75, and shake for $2.25. He leaves 15%, or $1.05, for a tip. How much money does Wesley have left?

   Wesley has _____ left.

5. 896 ÷ 2 =

Lesson 59

1. Fill in the blank with <, >, or = to make the number sentence true.

   $\dfrac{1}{5}$ _____ $\dfrac{7}{8}$

2. 456 x 8 =

3. 675 ÷ 5 =

4. 9 ÷ 9 =

5. On which coordinate is the smiley face located?

   _____

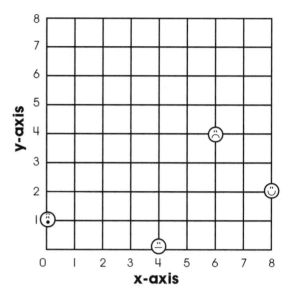

Lesson 60

1. Julie has 280 pairs of shoes in her closet. If $\dfrac{3}{5}$ of her shoes are sandals and the rest are tennis shoes, how many pairs of tennis shoes does Julie have in her closet?

   Julie has _____ pairs of tennis shoes in her closet.

2. 453 x 7 =

3. 336 ÷ 6 =

4. Fill in the blank with <, >, or = to make the number sentence true.

   $\dfrac{3}{5}$ _____ $\dfrac{3}{4}$

5. 543 x 23 =

Lesson 61

Name _____

1. Write the number in standard form.
900,000 + 80,000 + 500 + 7

_____

2. $433 \times 60 =$

3. $0.003 \times 62 =$

4. What would the letter "A" look like if it were rotated one-quarter turn to the right? Circle the letter beside the best answer.

A.   B.   C.

5. Lacy is moving on Saturday. She has packed 89 boxes in each room in her house. She has 5 rooms in her house. How many boxes has Lacy packed in all?

Lacy has packed a total of _____ boxes in all.

Lesson 62

1. Ramòn delivers 935 newspapers each week. He delivers newspapers Monday, Tuesday, Wednesday, Thursday, and Friday. He delivers the same number of newspapers each day. How many papers does Ramòn deliver each day?

Ramòn delivers _____ papers each week.

2. Estimate the answer. Round to the nearest ten thousand.
$67,545 - 33,878 =$

3. $907 \times 40 =$

4. $116 \div 4 =$

5. How many lines of symmetry does a rectangle have? _____

Lesson 63

1. Write the numbers in order from least to greatest.

   54,678   43,546   55,678   54,897   43,765

   _____

2. $234 \times 8 =$

3. Write the number in expanded form. 76,789

   _____

4. How many lines of symmetry does the letter U have? _____

5. Isabella wakes up at 8 A.M. on Saturday. She spends 20 minutes getting ready, 15 minutes helping her mom, and 30 minutes eating breakfast, then she leaves for her soccer game. What time does Isabella leave?

   Isabella leaves for her soccer game at _____.

Lesson 64

1. Which of the following pictures shows the arrow in the box rotated at a 90-degree angle? Circle the answer.

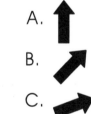

A.

B.

C.

2. $91 \times 7 =$

3. $96 \div 4 =$

4. Write the number in word form. 89,980

   _____

5. Samantha sent out 774 advertisements to try to get people to visit her ice cream stand. She forgot to stamp $\frac{1}{3}$ of the letters that she mailed. How many letters did Samantha forget to stamp?

   Samantha forgot to stamp _____ letters.

Lesson 65

1. Write the number in word form. 103,567

   _____

2. 657 x 10 =

3. 576 ÷ 2 =

4. 904 x 9 =

5. Write the numbers in order from greatest to least.
   705,098   750,546   775,987   750,654   705,908

   _____

Lesson 66

1. What motion was used to get from the first figure to the second figure?
   Circle the letter beside the best answer.
   A.   flip
   B.   turn
   C.   slide

2. 87 x 80 =

3. 56 ÷ 7 =

4. Write the number five hundred seventy-eight thousand, six hundred one
   on the line below.

   _____

5. Exactly 378 people visited a museum on Wednesday. Each person who
   visited the museum paid $0.75 admission. How much money was paid
   for admission on Wednesday?

   _____ was paid for admission on Wednesday.

Lesson 67

1. What move was made to get from the first figure to the second figure? Circle the letter beside the best answer.
   A. flip
   B. turn
   C. slide

   B   B

2. $342 \times 70 =$

3. $87 \div 3 =$

4. Jessie rides his bike 20 kilometers every week. How many kilometers does Jessie ride his bike in 8 weeks?

   Jessie rides his bike _____ kilometers in 8 weeks.

5. Write the number in standard form. $700,000 + 40,000 + 300 + 3$

   _____

Lesson 68

1. Write the number six hundred seventy-nine thousand, six hundred four.

   _____

2. During April, 287 people visited an amusement park. During May, 379 people visited the same amusement park. During June, twice as many people visited the amusement park as visited in April and May combined. How many people visited the amusement park in June?

   _____ people visited the amusement park in June.

3. $77 \times 80 =$

4. $105 \div 7 =$

5. How many lines of symmetry does a square have? _____

Lesson 69

1. Raùl earns $7.65 each time he baby-sits his little sister, Carla. If Raùl baby-sits Carla 9 times in August, how much money will he earn?

   Raùl will earn _____ in August.

2. Write the numbers in order from greatest to least.
   54,343   43,454   55,456   54,345

3. $774 \div 6 =$

4. $732 \times 65 =$

5. How many lines of symmetry does the bicycle have? _____

Lesson 70

1. Ben is stacking wood. He plans to stack 108 pieces of wood in each of 16 piles. How many pieces of wood will Ben use in all?

   Ben plans to stack a total of _____ pieces of wood.

2. $140 \div 4 =$

3. $567 \times 54 =$

4. Write the fractions in order from least to greatest. $\frac{4}{8}$ $\frac{2}{3}$ $\frac{1}{8}$ $\frac{1}{4}$

5. How many lines of symmetry does the triangle have? _____

Lesson 71

1. A total of 419 students will attend Field Day. Mr. Weaver needs 4 ribbons for each student and 48 ribbons for the parents who will be helping. How many ribbons does Mr. Weaver need in all?

    Mr. Weaver needs _____ ribbons in all.

2. Round each number to the nearest ten thousands place. Then, estimate your answer.

    $76,343 - 54,607 =$

3. Circle the thermometer that shows the warmest temperature.

4. $5,001 \times 6 =$

5. $486 \div 6 =$

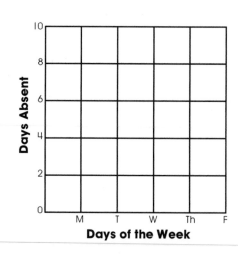

Lesson 72

1. Nancy, Jim, and Terrance collected 769 stickers during the school year. They want to divide the stickers equally. They plan to give any left over stickers to Vanessa. How many stickers will each person get?

    Nancy, Jim, and Terrance will each get _____ stickers.
    Vanessa will get _____ sticker(s).

2. $4,114 \times 8 =$

3. $1.05 \times 78 =$

4. $809 \times 55 =$

5. Manuel tracked his class's attendance for 1 week. Using the information below, make a line graph showing these results:

    Monday = 2   Thursday = 4
    Tuesday = 3   Friday = 0
    Wednesday = 3

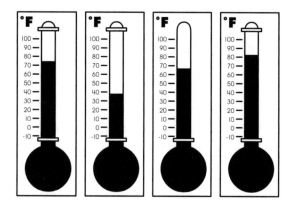

Lesson 73

1. Mrs. Blackburn has 33 students in her fourth grade class. Her students are making collages on Friday, so she brings in 5 magazines for each student. How many magazines does Mrs. Blackburn bring to class?

   Mrs. Blackburn brings _____ magazines to class.

2. 3.5 x 96 =

3. 60 ÷ 6 =

4. 881 x 47 =

5. The table shows the cost of going to the movies over the last 5 years. Based on the information provided in the table, how much do you think it will cost to attend a movie in Year 5?

Cost of Attending a Movie	
Year	Cost
1	$2.25
2	$3.00
3	$3.75
4	$4.50
5	

Lesson 74

1. If 98,876 people live in Johnson City, and 58,990 of the people who live in Johnson City are children, how many of the people who live in Johnson City are not children?

   _____ of the people who live in Johnson City are not children.

2. 765 x 26 =

3. 192 ÷ 12 =

4. 8,867 x 5 =

5. Based on the information in the graph, how many cookies did the 6th graders sell? Fill in the blank and finish the graph.

   The 6th graders sold _____ cookies.

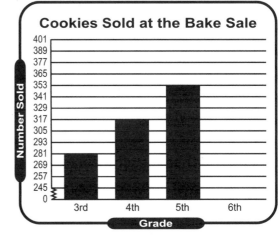

Cookies Sold at the Bake Sale

Lesson 75

1. During the year, Max travels 5,678 miles by airplane. He travels twice as many miles by train. How many miles does Max travel by train?

    Max travels _____ miles by train.

2. How many inches long is the calculator?

    The calculator measures _____ inches in length.

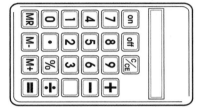

3. $2,002 \times 4 =$

4. $996 \times 22 =$

5. $784 \div 8 =$

Lesson 76

1. There are 180 days in the school year. Ellen has to walk 3 miles to her elementary school. If she was late $\frac{1}{2}$ of the school days, how many days was Ellen on time?

    Ellen was on time _____ days of the school year.

2. The line graph shows a list of the coldest winter days for a number of years. Based on the information presented in the line graph, which date was the coldest?

    _____

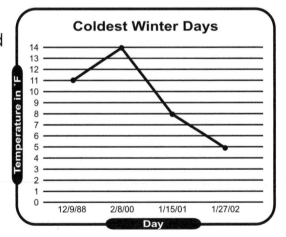

3. $728 \div 8 =$

4. $876 \times 47 =$

5. What is the perimeter of the triangle?

    _____ inches

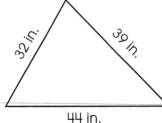

Lesson 77

1. What is the area of the rectangle? _____ feet^2

2. $6,567 \times 3 =$

3. $2,123 \times 4 =$

4. $8 \times 9 =$

5. There are 864 students enrolled at Cass Elementary School. Of those, 219 students signed up to play soccer. The coaches divided the students into 15 equal teams. How many students are on each team? How many students are left over?

There are _____ students on each team.
There are _____ students left over.

Lesson 78

1. What is the volume of the rectangular prism?

_____ cubic units

2. $3,456 \times 8 =$

3. James wants to figure out how long it will take him to do his chores. He will spend 45 minutes taking care of Mr. Siler's dog. Then, he will spend 25 minutes folding laundry. He will also spend 20 minutes cleaning his room. How long will it take James to do all of his chores?

It will take James _____ minutes to do all of his chores.

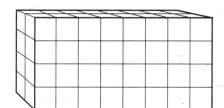

4. $876 \times 49 =$

5. Cynthia is measuring her brother's height. How tall is Cynthia's brother?

Cynthia's brother measures _____ feet tall.

Lesson 79

1. What is the volume of the cube?

   _____ cubic units

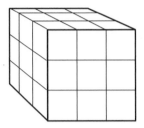

2. 4,345 x 18 =

3. 678 x 66 =

4. Which of the following units would be best to measure the length of an earthworm?

   inch   foot   yard   mile

5. If 664 people turn out to watch the parade, and $\frac{1}{4}$ of the people watching are wearing hats, how many people at the parade are not wearing hats?

   _____ people at the parade are not wearing hats.

Lesson 80

1. Lizzie works 7 hours a day, 7 days a week. How many hours does Lizzie work in 6 weeks?

   Lizzie works _____ hours in 6 weeks.

2. 607 x 83 =

3. 4,564 x 5 =

4. 1,002 ÷ 2 =

5. Determine the area of the rectangle. Include the unit of measurement in your answer.

12 ft.

19 ft.

Lesson 81

1. What figure does the item in the box most closely resemble?

   _____

2. 3,098 x 78 =

3. 768 ÷ 4 =

4. 1.75 x 69 =

5. Brenda is measuring the diameter of a wheel on her wagon. What is the diameter of the wagon wheel?

   _____

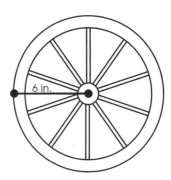

6 in.

Lesson 82

1. 4,012 ÷ 2 =

2. 289 x 78 =

3. 2,343 x 65 =

Use this information to answer questions 4 and 5. Ava's backyard is shaped like a square. It is 25 feet long and 25 feet wide.

4. What is the perimeter of Ava's backyard?

   _____

5. What is the area of Ava's backyard?

   _____

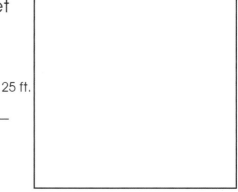

25 ft.

25 ft.

Lesson 83

For questions 1 and 2, label each figure a segment, ray, or line.

1. R •————————————▶ S   _____

2. G •————————————• R   _____

3. 2,345 x 9 =

4. 977 x 53 =

5. Mr. Thompson ordered new textbooks for his 4th graders. He received 89 boxes of textbooks. Each box of textbooks weighs 79 pounds, and there are 54 textbooks in each box. How many textbooks did Mr. Thompson order in all?

   Mr. Thompson ordered _____ textbooks in all.

Lesson 84

1. 483 ÷ 7 =

2. Jake is wrapping a present for his mom. The gift box he is wrapping is a rectangular prism. How many straight edges does a rectangular prism have?

   A rectangular prism has _____ straight edges.

3. 135 x 87 =

4. 9,004 x 2 =

5. What is the volume of the cube?

   _____ cubic units

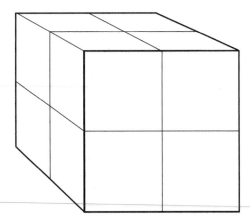

Lesson 85

1. 2,098 x 5 =

2. 7.75 x 97 =

3. 3.31 x 765 =

4. The 4th graders at Patton Elementary attended a special workshop on Wednesday. For an art activity, the visiting teacher divided the 240 students into 16 groups. How many children were in each group?

   There were _____ students in each group.

5. I am a 3-dimensional shape. I have 5 faces and 5 vertices. My faces consist of 2 different shapes. What shape am I?

   _____

Lesson 86

1. During the summer Hank, Jen, and Cindy each earned $237 doing odd jobs. They want to buy a basketball goal for their driveway, so they decided to save their money. The basketball goal that they want to buy costs $489. How much more money do Hank, Jen, and Cindy need to save altogether in order to make their purchase?

   Altogether, they need to save _____ more to make their purchase.

2. 2,013 x 52 =

3. 675 ÷ 3 =

4. 840 ÷ 12 =

5. Leanne is planting a garden in the shape of a rectangle. Based on the picture, what is the area of the garden that Leanne is planting? Include the unit of measure in your answer.

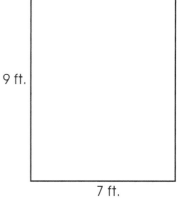

9 ft.

7 ft.

Lesson 87

1.   3,234 x 45 =

2.   1,234 x 22 =

3.   Desmond wakes up at 9:15 A.M. It takes him 35 minutes to fold 4 loads of laundry, 35 minutes to bathe the dog, 45 minutes to bake brownies, and 1 hour to mow the lawn. After he finishes all of his chores, he sits down to rest. What time does Desmond sit down to rest?

      Desmond sits down to rest at _____.

4.   2,313 ÷ 9 =

5.   Estimate the circumference of the circle.

      The circumference of the circle is
      about _____ feet

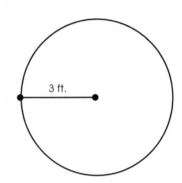

Lesson 88

1.   There are 315 kids in the Legend Oaks subdivision. If $\frac{1}{3}$ of the kids ride their bikes to school and the rest of the kids walk, how many kids walk to school?

      _____ kids walk to school.

2.   72 ÷ 8 =

3.   45,565 – 34,897 =

4.   7,899 x 6 =

5.   Look at the angle. Circle the answer
      that best describes the angle.

      right   obtuse   acute

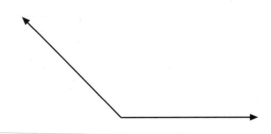

Lesson 89

1. Mr. Ogle buys 4,522 pencils at the beginning the year. He gives an equal number of pencils to teachers in the third, fourth, fifth, and sixth grades. He keeps the remaining pencils in his office. How many pencils does Mr. Ogle give to each grade level? How many extra pencils does he have in his office?

   He gives the teachers in each grade level _____ pencils and has _____ pencils remaining in his office.

2. 1.90 x 38 =

3. 543 x 89 =

4. 5,784 x 9 =

5. Find the diameter of the circle to estimate the circumference.
   diameter = _____ centimeters
   circumference ≈ _____ centimeters

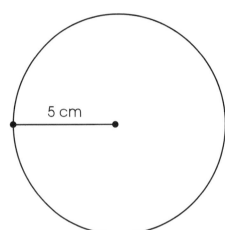

5 cm

Lesson 90

1. Abby bought 182 cases of water for her restaurant. There are 24 bottles of water in each case. How many bottles of water did Abby buy in all?

   Abby bought _____ bottles of water in all.

2. 54.4 x 3.0 =

3. 32.6 x 98 =

4. 7,432 x 3 =

5. What is the volume of the rectangular prism?

   _____ cubic units

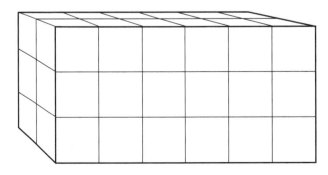

Lesson 91

1. If the current year is 2004, and James was born in 1975, Louis was born in 1981, and Forrest was born in 1983, how old is James? How many years older is James than Forrest?

   In 2004, James is _____ years old, and is _____ years older than Forrest.

2. (2 x 12) divided by 4 =

3. 34,432 – 12,997 =

4. 204 ÷ 12 =

5. Draw an object in the box that has at least two lines of symmetry.

Lesson 92

1. The public library has 3,039 books for elementary students. Of those, $\frac{1}{3}$ of the books are at the fourth grade reading level. How many of the books are at the fourth grade reading level?

   _____ of the books are at the fourth grade reading level.

2. 763 ÷ 7 =

3. 81,765 – 34,769 =

4. 14 x b = 84   b = _____

5. Circle the acute angle.

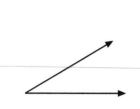

Lesson 93

1. In June, Lee travels 1,765 miles. In July, he traveled twice as far as in June. How many miles did Lee travel in July?

   Lee traveled _____ miles in July.

2. (76 x 81) divided by 3 =

3. 189 x 97 =

4. 4,566 ÷ 6 =

5. Circle the word that correctly describes the relationship between Pentagon A and Pentagon B.

   rotation   proportion   translation

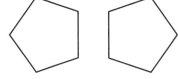

Pentagon A   Pentagon B

Lesson 94

1. Beka has $1.10 in her pocket. She has 5 coins. What combination of coins might Beka have in her pocket?

   _____

2. Six cubes have _____ faces and _____ edges.

3. 279 x 41 =

Look at the spinner to answer questions 4 and 5.

4. On what color or colors is the spinner least likely to land?

   _____

5. On what color or colors is the spinner most likely to land?

   _____

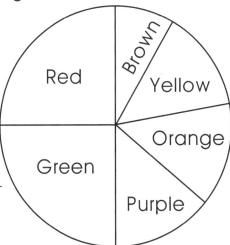

Lesson 95

1. Delia has 238 cookbooks. Each cookbook is between 50 and 100 pages long. What is the lowest possible total number of pages for all 238 cookbooks combined? What is the highest possible total number of pages in all 238 cookbooks combined?

   The lowest possible total number of pages is _____.
   The highest possible total number of pages is _____.

2. Circle the triangle that shows a line of symmetry.

3. 876 x 91 =

4. (678 x 4) divided by 2 =

5. 2,028 ÷ 2 =

Lesson 96

1. Students from 5 schools are competing in a baseball tournament. Exactly 200 students from each school want to play. Each team will have 10 players. If all the students get to play in the tournament, how many teams will compete in the tournament?

   _____ teams will compete in the tournament.

2. 7,987 x 1 =

3. 4,876 x 6 =

4. 783 ÷ 9 =

5. Write the names of 2 three-dimensional shapes that have curved surfaces.

   _____

   _____

Lesson 97

1. The mayor of Glenview Heights gave 3 flags to every person in his community. There are 1,298 people living in Glenview Heights. How many flags did the mayor give away in all?

   The mayor gave away a total of _____ flags.

2. 2,005 x 5 =

3. (876 x 56) divided by 7 =

4. 345 x 213 =

5. Circle the shape that is congruent to the shape in the box.

Lesson 98

1. Carrie has $0.79 in her wallet. What kinds of coins does Carrie have? Write 2 different possible coin combinations on the lines below.

   _____

   _____

2. 56,877 – 45,996 =

3. 588 ÷ 12 =

4. 780 x 89 =

5. Look at the following pattern, or net. If you cut out and folded the net, what 3-dimensional figure would you have?

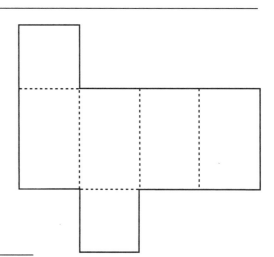

Lesson 99

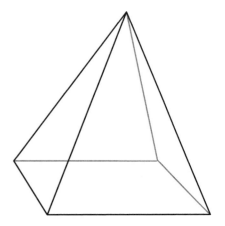

1. Count the number of vertices on the square pyramid.

    The square pyramid has _____ vertices.

2. 6,765 x 8 =

3. 15 x n = 135   n = _____

4. 78,887 – 67,889 =

5. There are 6,548 cowboy hats for sale at Cowboy Central and $\frac{1}{4}$ of the hats for sale have feathers. The rest of the hats do not have feathers. How many of the hats do not have feathers?

    _____ of the hats do not have feathers.

Lesson 100

1. Melissa needs 1 hour and 35 minutes to complete her homework. She starts working on her homework at 3:15 P.M. What time will Melissa finish her homework?

    Melissa will finish her homework at _____.

2. 8,767 x 8 =

3. (33 x 33) divided by 3 =

4. 9 x 8 =

5. Selena wants to describe the shape of a cube to her friend, Hector. Without using the word "cube," help Selena by writing a sentence describing the shape of a cube. Think about sides, faces, and vertices.

    _____

    _____

Lesson 101

1. Jake weighs 54 pounds. Liz weighs 62 pounds. Their father, Jim, weighs twice as much as Jake and Liz combined. How much does Jim weigh?

   Jim weighs _____ pounds.

2. (14 x 13) divided by 2 =

3. 3,564 x 8 =

4. 5,897 − 3,456 =

5. Find the perimeter of the octagon. Include the unit of measure in your answer.

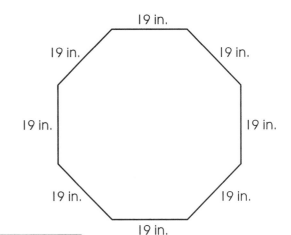

_____

Lesson 102

1. 0.75 x 300 =

2. Melody has $.75 in her pocket. She has 10 coins. What combination of coins might Melody have in her pocket?

   _____

3. (56 x 9) divided by 4 =

4. 875 ÷ 7 =

5. Use a ruler to find the length, in centimeters, of the crayon.

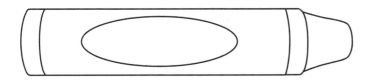

   The crayon is _____ centimeters long.

Daily Math Warm-Ups Grade 4

Lesson 103

1. 761 x 388 =

2. Libby is helping her mom set up for her brother's birthday party. Her brother's party starts at 4 P.M. Libby knows that they will need 1 hour to get the goody bags ready, 45 minutes to stuff the piñata, and 1 hour to decorate the cake. At what time should Libby and her mom start getting ready for the party?

    Libby and her mom should start getting ready for the party at _____.

3. (2,286 – 1,989) x 9 =

4. 2 miles = _____ feet

5. Use your ruler to measure the length, in centimeters, of the thumbtack.

    _____

Lesson 104

1. 467 x 675 =

2. 7,767 ÷ 9 =

3. 67,876 – 66,569 =

4. 15 feet = _____ yards

5. A department store has 4,572 coffee mugs for sale. There is an equal number of red, green, blue, yellow, orange, and red mugs. The cost of each mug is $6.75. How many blue mugs are for sale at the store?

    _____ blue mugs are for sale at the store.

Lesson 105

1. The admission price to the Dellview Carnival is $1.25. If 789 students attend the carnival, what is the total that all 789 students together paid to enter the carnival?

   All 789 students together paid a total of _____.

2. 765 x 876 =

3. 8 feet = _____ inches

4. 2,110 ÷ 10 =

5. Circle the unit of measure that would best describe the length of a dump truck.

   meter   centimeter

   kilometer   ton

Lesson 106

1. $(7,876 - 5,879) \times 7 =$

2. 7,984 ÷ 8 =

3. 12 x 9 =

4. 100 meters = _____ centimeters

5. Jeremy travels 16 miles total to and from school every day. How many miles does Jeremy travel to and from school in 20 school days?

   Jeremy travels a total distance of _____ miles in 20 school days.

Lesson 107

1. Jon mows 1 lawn every day for 17 days. He earns $5.50 for each lawn mowed. How much money has Jon earned after 17 days?

    Jon has earned _____ after 17 days.

2. About how much water will the bucket hold? Circle the best answer.

    10 inches
    10 pints
    10 quarts
    10 gallons

3. 300,987 – 67,870 =

4. (183 x 65) divided by 5 =

5. What is the best unit of measurement to use to determine the weight of the boy? Circle the best answer.

    ounce   yard   pound   inch

Lesson 108

1. 769 x 55 =

2. 6,824 ÷ 8 =

3. 600 ÷ 3 =

4. 5 years = _____ months

5. What temperature is shown on the thermometer?

    _____

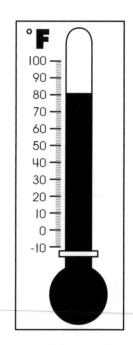

Lesson 109

1. Samantha went out to eat with her friends on Monday, Tuesday, Wednesday, and Friday. She spent $5.65 on Monday, $7.50 on Tuesday, $9.75 on Wednesday, and $5.95 on Friday. How much more money did Samantha spend on Wednesday and Friday than on Monday and Tuesday?

    Samantha spent _____ more on Wednesday and Friday.

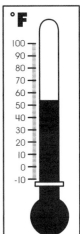

2. (16 x 15) divided by 30 =

3. 407 x 69 =

4. 4 centimeters = _____ millimeters

5. About what temperature is shown on the thermometer? Circle the letter beside the best answer.

    A. 47°   B. 54°   C. 62°   D. 73°

Lesson 110

1. Circle the unit that would best describe the capacity of a milk jug.

    gallon   millimeter   inch   pound

2. (876 – 765) x 18 =

3. 9 x 11 =

4. Dena has 481 photo albums. There are 107 photos in each album. How many photos are in all of the photo albums combined?

    There are _____ photos in all of the photo albums combined.

5. Look at the picture. What is the length of the pencil?

    _____

Lesson 111

1. Larry is going on a trip to San Diego with his mom. His plane departs at
    9:20 A.M. He needs to arrive at the airport 2 hours and 45 minutes before
    his plane leaves. What time does Larry need to get to the airport?

    Larry needs to arrive at the airport at _____.

2. 6 hours = _____ minutes

3. 397 x 78 =

4. 544 ÷ 16 =

5. (27 x 6) divided by 9 =

Lesson 112

1. 297 x 49 =

2. Fill in the blank with <, >, or= to make the number sentence true.
    678,990 _____ 678,009

3. 4 years = _____ months

4. 179 x 564 =

5. Mary is making cookies for her holiday
    party. She adds 2 cups of flour to
    each dozen cookies. How many cups of
    flour should Mary add to make 8 dozen
    batches of cookies? Use the chart to
    help you find the solution.

    Mary needs to add _____ cups of
    flour to make 8 dozen cookies.

Baking Chart	
Amount of Cookies	Cups of Flour
1 dozen	2
3 dozen	6
5 dozen	10
7 dozen	14

Lesson 113

1. The basketball team plays 114 games during the season. Each game lasts 2 hours. How many hours does the team spend playing basketball games during the season?

    The team spends _____ hours playing basketball games during the season.

2. Circle the most reasonable estimate of the weight of a paper clip.

    1 liter   1 gram   1 inch   1 milliliter

3. 701 x 495 =

4. 3 meters = _____ centimeters

5. Look at the thermometer. Circle the word that best describes the temperature.

    warm   cool   freezing   hot

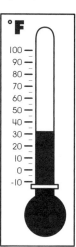

Lesson 114

1. A photo shop needs to develop 7,896 rolls of film over a 2-day period. They want to develop an equal number of rolls of film each day. How many rolls of film should the photo shop develop each day?

    The photo shop should develop _____ photos each day.

2. 5,608 ÷ 8 =

3. 696 x 302 =

4. 578 x 676 =

5. What is the area of the triangle? Include the unit of measure in your answer.

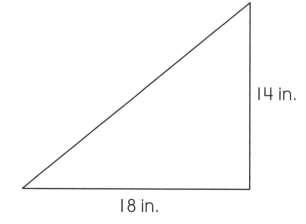

14 in.

18 in.

Lesson 115

1. Adam runs a distance of 140 miles over a 10-day period. It takes Adam about 9 minutes to run each mile. If Adam runs an equal number of miles each day, how many miles does Adam run each day?

    Adam runs a distance of _____ miles each day.

2. 1,236 ÷ 6 =

3. 78,008 − 76,980 =

4. 4,000 grams = _____ kilograms

5. Determine the volume of the shape.

    _____ cubic units

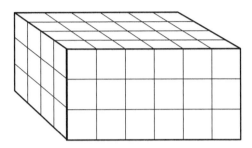

Lesson 116

1. The post office is open from 8 A.M. to 5 P.M. every day. On Thursday, 3,645 letters were mailed from the post office. An equal number of letters were mailed every hour. How many letters were mailed each hour the post office was open?

    _____ letters were mailed each hour the post office was open.

2. 589 x 90 =

3. 6,225 ÷ 5 =

4. (56 x 432) − 794 =

5. Determine the perimeter of the shape.

    _____ cm

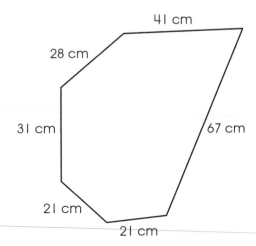

41 cm
28 cm
31 cm
67 cm
21 cm
21 cm

Lesson 117

1. Look at the thermometers. At which temperature would you most likely wear a sweater? _____

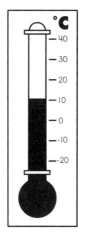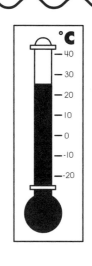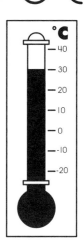

2. $9{,}096 \div 8 =$

3. $22{,}110 - 21{,}110 =$

4. $345 \times 675 =$

5. How many inches long is the nail?

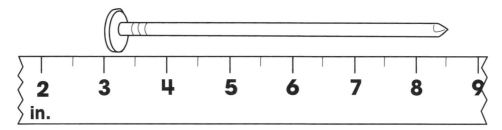

The nail is _____ inches long.

Lesson 118

1. Exactly 2,015 kids play in the Julian Soccer League. The children are divided into 5 age categories, between the ages of 5 and 12. Each age category has an equal number of players. How many players are in each age category?

   There are _____ players in each age category.

2. 30 centimeters = _____ millimeters

3. (45×88) divided by $6 =$

4. $402 \times 414 =$

5. Which of the following is the most likely height of a hot chocolate mug?

   5 inches   5 feet   5 miles   5 cups

Lesson 119

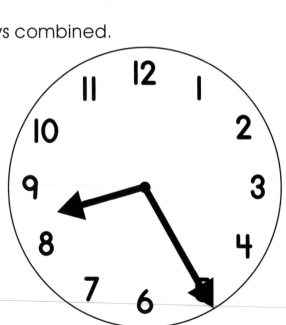

1. A large company receives 19,004 telephone calls on Monday, 18,976 calls on Tuesday, and 18,090 calls on Wednesday. How many more calls did the company receive on Monday than on Wednesday?

   The company received _____ more calls on Wednesday.

2. Fill in the blank with <, >, or = to make the number sentence true.
   78,009 _____ 79,008

3. $344 \times 89 =$

4. 5 quarts = _____ pints

5. $675 \times 897 =$

Lesson 120

1. Anya baby-sits 4 Saturdays in a row. Each Saturday, she earns $10.75. How much money does Anya earn in all 4 Saturdays combined?

   Anya earns _____ in all 4 Saturdays combined.

2. $8,981 \div 7 =$

3. $(97 \times 64) + 4,567 =$

4. $250 \times 67 =$

5. Look at the clock. The time is 8:25 P.M. What time will it be in 2 hours and 35 minutes?

   _____

Name _____

Lesson 121

1. Jamal stamped 5,768 envelopes each day on Monday, on Tuesday, on Thursday, on Friday, and also on Saturday. How many envelopes did Jamal stamp over all 5 days?

   Jamal stamped a total of _____ envelopes over all 5 days.

2. Circle the largest fraction.

   $\dfrac{2}{2}$ $\dfrac{2}{3}$ $\dfrac{2}{8}$ $\dfrac{2}{9}$

3. $100,989 - 34,675 =$

4. (67×84) divided by $6 =$

5. $786 \times 76 =$

Lesson 122

1. A group of 4 friends divided 4,568 marbles equally between them. The marbles are red, yellow, orange, and blue. How many marbles did each friend get?

   Each friend got _____ marbles.

2. $704 \times 266 =$

3. Write the number in standard form.
   seven million, eight hundred thousand, sixty-one

   _____

4. $3,765 \div 1 =$

5. $156 \times 543 =$

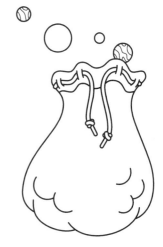

Lesson 123

1. Put the numbers in order from greatest to least.
71,323   65,655   70,656   17,987

_____

2. Write the number in word form. 54,876

_____

3. Marty has $54.50. Her brother has twice as much money. How much money does Marty's brother have?

Marty's brother has _____.

4. 289 x 876 =

5. Circle the figure that is not a quadrilateral.

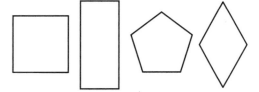

Lesson 124

1. Put the numbers in order from least to greatest.
18,879   18,989   18,009   81,234

_____

2. 802 x 78 =

3. (56 x 67) x 9 =

4. Randy has $187.98 in his bank account. He receives a gift of $55.00 from his grandmother for his birthday. Then, he spends $18.75 on a new music CD. How much money does Randy have left?

Randy has _____ left.

5. Look at the angle below. Circle the word that best describes the angle.

obtuse   right
equilateral   acute

Lesson 125

1. Circle the even numbers.

   43,565   32,678   23,679   98,000

2. Sherrie saves $2,458. She wants to invest $\frac{1}{2}$ the money and put the rest in her savings account. How much money should Sherrie invest?

   Sherrie should invest _____.

3. $2,331 \div 21 =$

4. $620 \times 876 =$

5. Circle the triangle that is not congruent to the triangle in the box.

Lesson 126

1. Put the numbers in order from greatest to least.
   101,543   112,878   101,565   111,987

   _____

2. Danielle put $78.95 in the bank. Her brother put 3 times as much money in the bank. Her sister put $\frac{1}{3}$ as much money in the bank. How much money did Danielle's brother put in the bank?

   Danielle's brother put _____ in the bank.

3. $513 \times 765 =$

4. $809,876 - 456,987 =$

5. How many vertices do 5 pentagons have? _____ vertices

Lesson 127

1. Leah has 5,679 beads. She uses $\frac{1}{3}$ of her beads for a necklace and saves the rest of her beads for another project. How many beads does Leah save for another project?

   Leah saves _____ beads for another project.

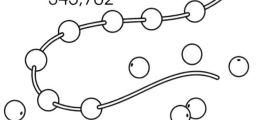

2. Circle the odd numbers.

   67,876   45,675   102,673   345,762

3. $786,987 - 43,786 =$

4. $467 \times 87 =$

5. $3,766 \div 7 =$

Lesson 128

1. Jeffrey counts the edges of 2 signs in his neighborhood. The first sign is an octagon and the second sign is a hexagon. How many sides do both signs together have?

   Both signs together have _____ sides.

2. $897 \times 879 =$

3. $49,987 - 897 =$

4. $287 \times 0.98 =$

5. Write the number two hundred fifty-eight thousand, six hundred eight.

   _____

Lesson 129

1. Henry finds 86 shells on the beach on Tuesday. On Wednesday, he finds $\frac{1}{2}$ as many shells. On Thursday, he finds 3 times as many shells as he did on Wednesday. How many shells did Henry find on Thursday?

   Henry found _____ shells on Thursday.

2. $9,878 \times 8 =$

3. $4,563 \div 9 =$

4. $(54,878 + 458,897) - 45,009 =$

5. Put the numbers in order from greatest to least.
   51,987   54,456   54,666   55,098

Lesson 130

1. Will, Jan, and Greg are going to the movies. They have a total of $26. Greg has the most money. Jan has twice as much money as Will. Greg has $11. How much money does Jan have?

   Jan has _____.

2. $201 \times 212 =$

3. $1,896 \div 12 =$

4. Write the number three hundred fifty thousand, seven.

   _____

5. Circle the largest odd number.

   123,232   145,675   198,098   166,345   198,000

Lesson 131

1. The table shows the number of refrigerators that were sold at Rachel's Refrigerators during the first 6 months of the year. How many more refrigerators were sold in January, February, and March than in April, May, and June?

   _____ more refrigerators were sold in January, February, and March than in April, May, and June.

2. 189 x 79 =

3. 182 ÷ 14 =

4. 6.78 x 76 =

Refrigerators Sold	
Month	**Units Sold**
January	112
February	232
March	181
April	98
May	189
June	137

5. Tracy, Kim, and Allie each saved $64 to buy a new CD player. When they put their money together, they had saved twice as much money as the CD player costs. They decided to give half of their money to charity. How much money did the sisters give to charity?

   The sisters gave _____ to charity.

Lesson 132

1. Look at the bar graph. How many more children rode the bus during Weeks 2 and 5 than during Weeks 1 and 4?

   _____ more children rode the bus during Weeks 2 and 5 than during Weeks 1 and 4.

2. 324 ÷ 18 =

3. 187 x 876 =

4. 0.98 x 786 =

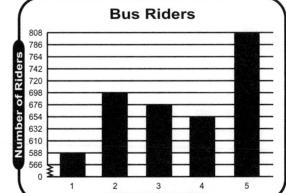

5. Dan had $20. He spent $7.75 on dinner and $11.50 on flowers for his mom. How much money does Dan have now?

   Dan has _____ now.

Lesson 133

1. Marshall is moving to Toronto. He packs 168 comic books into 8 different boxes. He packs an equal number of comic books in each box. How many comic books does Marshall pack into each box?

   Marshall packs _____ comic books into each box.

2. 401 x 765 =

3. 68,987 – 56,987 =

4. 564 x 87 =

5. Look at the pictograph. How many cookies did Erin bake during the entire week?

   Erin baked a total of _____ cookies.

Batches of Cookies Baked by Erin

= 12 cookies

Mon.	(4 cookies)
Tues.	(8 cookies)
Wed.	(5 cookies)
Thurs.	(9 cookies)
Fri.	(8 cookies)

Lesson 134

1. The tally chart shows the number of each color of scarf sold at Willy's Warm Wear during February. How many more gray and blue scarves were sold than green and purple scarves?

   _____ more gray and blue scarves were sold than green and purple scarves.

2. 161 x 89 =

3. 129 x 16 =

4. 495 ÷ 15 =

5. Each item in the vending machine costs $0.75. Ethan buys 5 items from the vending machine. How much money does Ethan spend?

   Ethan spends a total of _____.

Scarves Sold at Willy's Warm Wear

Red	Blue	Green	Purple	Gray
ͰͰͰ ͰͰͰ ͰͰͰ |||	ͰͰͰ ͰͰͰ ͰͰͰ |||	ͰͰͰ ͰͰͰ ||||	ͰͰͰ ͰͰͰ ͰͰͰ |||	ͰͰͰ ͰͰͰ ͰͰͰ ͰͰͰ ͰͰͰ	

Lesson 135

1. Exactly 45,768 people currently live in Rockville. In 10 years, there will be 3,765 more people living in Rockville. How many people will live in Rockville in 10 years?

   _____ people will live in Rockville in 10 years.

2. $2,000 \div 10 =$

3. $69,987 - 14,678 =$

4. $208 \times 768 =$

5. The pictograph shows the number of tickets sold for a popular movie. How many people attended the movie on Sunday?

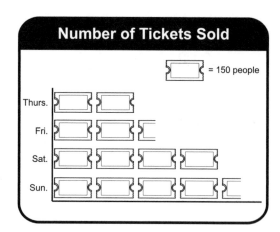

Number of Tickets Sold

= 150 people

Thurs.	
Fri.	
Sat.	
Sun.	

   _____ people attended the movie on Sunday.

Lesson 136

1. Dez has 840 tapes. She divides the tapes equally along 12 shelves. How many tapes does Dez put on each shelf?

   Dez puts _____ tapes on each shelf.

2. $7,648 \div 8 =$

3. $549 \times 876 =$

4. $186 \div 6 =$

5. The table shows the number of girls and boys in Grades 3, 4, and 5 enrolled in afternoon piano classes. What is the total number of boys taking piano in Grades 3, 4, and 5 combined?

Number of Boys and Girls in Piano Classes

Grade	Boys	Girls
3	15	17
4	21	16
5	24	28

   _____ boys are taking piano in Grades 3, 4, and 5 combined.

Lesson 137

1. The bar graph shows the average number of cars that passed through the Mulberry Street intersection at 5 different times of day. What is the average of the number of cars that passed through at 12 noon, 6 P.M., and 9 P.M.?

   An average of _____ cars passed through at 12 noon, 6 P.M., and 9 P.M.

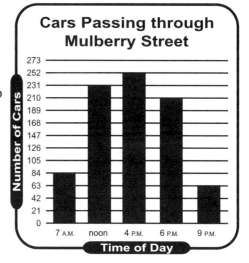

2. 901 x 55 =

3. 567 ÷ 21 =

4. 987 x 876 =

5. Jamie does 88 jumping jacks every 5 minutes. How many jumping jacks does Jamie do in 20 minutes?

   Jamie does _____ jumping jacks in 20 minutes.

Lesson 138

1. Louise buys 2,142 bottles of water for field day. If $\frac{1}{3}$ of the water is consumed between 8 A.M. and 11 A.M., how many bottles of water are consumed between 8 A.M. and 11 A.M.?

   _____ bottles of water are consumed between 8 A.M. and 11 A.M.

2. 9.98 x 76 =

3. 44.9 x 887 =

4. 876 x 543 =

5. The line graph shows the number of inches of rain during 4 months in a major city. Which month had $\frac{1}{2}$ as much rain as May?

   _____ had $\frac{1}{2}$ as much rain as May.

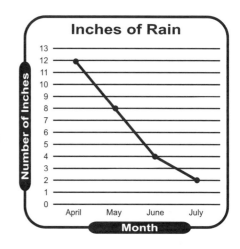

Lesson 139

1. There are 24 students in the gym class. The students divide 120 balls equally among themselves. How many balls does each student get?

    Each student gets _____ balls.

2. 1.59 x 44 =

3. 708 x 67 =

4. 85 x 66 =

5. The pictograph shows the number of pairs of sneakers sold. How many individual sneakers (not pairs of sneakers) were sold on Sunday?

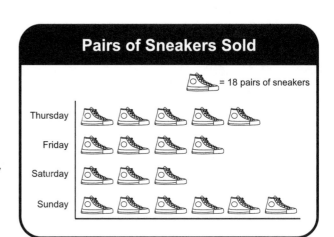

    _____ individual sneakers were sold on Sunday.

Lesson 140

1. The bar graph shows the number of days Liza spent at the beach each month. Sarah went to the beach $\frac{1}{2}$ as much as Liza during May and June. How many days did Sarah go to the beach during May and June?

    Sarah went to the beach _____ days during May and June.

2. 16.8 x 897 =

3. 0.96 x 76 =

4. 784 ÷ 8 =

5. Sal's Pizzeria has 708 chairs. There are 4 chairs at each table. How many tables are in the restaurant?

    There are _____ tables in Sal's Pizzeria.

Lesson 141

1. Round each number to the nearest hundred thousand. Then, estimate the answer.
532,453 – 456,755 is about _____ .

2. Round each number to the nearest hundred. Then, estimate the answer.
789 x 564 is about _____ .

3. Fill in the missing numbers to complete the pattern.
42, 126, 378, _____, _____, 10,206

4. 786 x 34 =

5. Eleanor has 3,524 coins. She wants to put an equal number of coins in 12 jars. She will give any remaining coins to her cousin. How many coins should Eleanor put in each jar? How many coins, if any, should she give to her cousin?

Eleanor should put _____ coins in each jar.
She should give _____ coins to her cousin.

Lesson 142

1. 807 x 59 =

2. 403 x 27 =

3. 3,200 ÷ 16 =

4. Last Tuesday, 780 different groups of people toured the Natural Science Center. Each group consisted of 15 people. In all, how many people toured the Natural Science Center on Tuesday?

In all, _____ people toured the Natural Science Center on Tuesday.

5. Fill in the missing numbers to complete the pattern.
1,278, 1,128, 978, _____, _____, 528, _____

Lesson 143

Name _____

1. A total of 599 pieces of paper are sitting on Mr. Duncan's desk. First, he divides the papers into 19 equal stacks. Then, he throws any extra paper in the recycling bin. How many pieces of paper are in each stack? How many, if any, extra pieces of paper does Mr. Duncan throw in the recycling bin?

    There are _____ pieces of paper in each stack.
    Mr. Duncan throws _____ pieces of paper in the recycling bin.

2. Round each number to the nearest ten thousands place. Then, estimate the answer.
    $65,567 - 45,654$ is about _____ .

3. $456 \times 789 =$

4. $1,764 \div 9 =$

5. Put an X through all of the odd numbers in the box.

234,459	234,345
21,456	
34,677	125,780

Lesson 144

1. $159 \times 123 =$

2. $1,001 \div 13 =$

3. Fill in the missing numbers to complete the pattern.
    901, 1,013 1,125, 1,237, _____, _____

4. $546 \times 76 =$

5. Toshi read 21 books each month last year. There are 12 months in a year. Each book that Toshi read was between 58 and 108 pages long. How many books total did Toshi read last year?

    Toshi read a total of _____ books last year.

Lesson 145

1. Round each number to the nearest ten thousand.
   54,675   _____
   34,234   _____
   134,567   _____
   89,098   _____

2. Allison saved $456.00 during March. She saved $\frac{1}{2}$ as much money during April. During May, she spent $178.95 on a plane ticket to visit her grandmother. How much money does Allison have now?

   Allison has _____ now.

3. 8,876 x 12 =

4. 4,000 ÷ 10 =

5. Fill in the missing numbers to complete the pattern.
   345, 326, 307, 288, _____, _____, _____

Lesson 146

1. Round each number to the nearest hundred thousands place.
   345,789 _____   321,123 _____
   980,876 _____   897,655 _____

2. 23,456 – 19,001 =

3. 234 ÷ 18 =

4. Oliver attended 176 days of school last year. He brought his lunch exactly $\frac{1}{4}$ of the days that he attended school. On the remaining days, he bought lunch in the school cafeteria. How many days did Oliver buy lunch?

   Oliver bought lunch in the school cafeteria on _____ days.

5. Jessica has one $10 bill and two $5 bills in her purse. She buys a new book for $5.75, a new pair of earrings for $6.55, and a gift for her best friend for $5.95. How much money does Jessica have left in her purse?

   Jessica has _____ left in her purse.

Lesson 147

1. 789 x 499 =

2. Round each number to the nearest millions place.
    1,234,675 _____
    2,564,987 _____
    1,765,998 _____

3. (78 x 67) – 3,098 =

4. Fill in the missing numbers to complete the pattern.
    789, 777, 780, 768, 771, _____, _____, _____

5. A total of 3,000 chairs are set up outside for a high school graduation.
    The chairs are set up in rows of 20 chairs each. How many rows of
    chairs are set up for the high school graduation?

    _____ rows of chairs are set up for the high school graduation.

Lesson 148

1. 745 x 445 =

2. 984 ÷ 8 =

3. 3,430 ÷ 5 =

4. Fill in the missing letters to complete the pattern.
    Z, A, X, C, V, E, _____, _____

5. Every day at the Alamance Airport, 600 airplanes land. An equal
    number of airplanes land between the hours of 6 A.M. and 9 P.M. How
    many airplanes land each hour at
    the Alamance Airport?

    _____ airplanes land each
    hour at the Alamance Airport.

Lesson 149

1. Round each number to the nearest thousands place.
    3,234   _____
    13,543   _____
    145,765   _____
    4,509   _____

2. 454 x 32 =

3. 360 ÷ 6 =

4. Fill in the missing numbers to complete the pattern.
    256, 286, 271, 301, 286, _____, _____, _____

5. A large mailing company mails 18,987 letters on Wednesday and
    16,786 letters on Friday. If 4,897 letters are returned, how many letters
    are not returned?

    _____ letters are not returned.

Lesson 150

1. A gathering of 476 families listened to a concert on Sunday. Each
    family spent $2.50 for admission. How much money total did all
    476 families spend?

    All 476 families spent _____ total.

2. 716 x 90 =

3. 233 x 54 =

4. 1,428 ÷ 7 =

5. Draw the missing shapes to complete the pattern.

Name _____

Lesson 151

1. There are 4,582 lightbulbs in a large department store. If $\frac{1}{2}$ of the lightbulbs don't work, how many of the lightbulbs need to be replaced?

    _____ of the lightbulbs need to be replaced.

2. Write the number seven million, six hundred thirty-three thousand, fourteen.

    _____

3. Circle the largest number.
    234,765   234,566   237,876   29,987

4. 4,002 x 7 =

5. (100 x 25) divided by 5 =

Lesson 152

1. 4,345 x 56 =

2. Round each number to the nearest ten thousand. Estimate the answer.
    67,876 – 55,897 is about _____ .

3. 118 x 44 =

4. Write the number in word form. 560,654

    _____

5. A train leaves the station at 7 A.M. The train consists of 87 passenger cars. There are 136 passengers riding in each passenger car. How many passengers are riding on the train?

    _____ passengers are riding on the train.

Lesson 153

1. $0.45 \times 876 =$

2. Rosalie bought 18 passes to Thrills and Chills Amusement Park. The passes cost $5.75 each. How much money did Rosalie spend in all?

   Rosalie spent a total of _____.

3. $144n = 1,296$ $n =$ _____

4. $456 \times 765 =$

5. Circle the smallest number.
   56,432   54,564   55,432   54,323

Lesson 154

1. There are 2,421 people performing in the Big Top Circus. The performers break up into 3 equal groups and eat dinner at different times. How many performers eat dinner at each different time?

   _____ performers eat dinner at each different time.

2. Use the clues to write the mystery 5-digit number. Each digit in the number is an odd number between 1 and 9. The number in the ten thousands place is 9. The number in the ones place and the tens place is the same. The number in the hundreds place and thousands place is the same. The number in the ones place is greater than 1, but less than 5. The number in the hundreds place is 2 less than 9. What is the number?

   The mystery number is _____.

3. $4,564 \div 7 =$

4. (45×76) divided by $4 =$

5. Put the numbers in order from least to greatest.
   45,456   44,565   46,567   45,675

Lesson 155

1. Jerry needs to read a 168-page book for class on Tuesday. He plans to spend all day Monday reading. He plans to read between 8:00 A.M. and 12:00 noon, and between 1:00 P.M. and 5:00 P.M. He plans to read an equal number of pages each hour. How many pages does Jerry plan to read each hour?

   Jerry plans to read _____ pages each hour.

2. Circle the smallest even number.

   80,879   800,987   88,768   80,876

3. $4,345 \times 6 =$

4. $981 \times 76 =$

5. $78,765 - 76,898 =$

Lesson 156

1. $2,456 \times 7 =$

2. $3,780 \div 7 =$

3. A new movie was showing on Friday at 11:00 A.M., 3:30 P.M., 6:45 P.M., 7:35 P.M., and 9:45 P.M. A total of 9,875 people saw the movie on Friday. An equal number of people saw each showing. How many people saw each showing?

   _____ people saw each showing.

4. $5,000 \div 5 =$

5. Write the number in word form. 144,657

   _____

   _____

Lesson 157

1. 8.90 x 555 =

2. 8,867 x 9 =

3. 2.22 x 7 =

4. Write the number three million, seven hundred eighteen thousand, six hundred twelve.

_____

5. A new company printed 345,345 magazines in its first year of operation. In its second year, the company printed 564,657 magazines. How many more magazines did it print in its second year of operation?

The company printed _____ more magazines in its second year than in its first year.

Lesson 158

1. Write the number in word form. 12,234,000

_____

2. 6,544 x 9 =

3. Jeremy earned $486.55 mowing lawns and $244.67 baby-sitting. Later, he received a check for $150.00 from his grandparents for his birthday. He bought a new video game for $79.95 and a skateboard for $138.00. How much money does Jeremy have left?

Jeremy has _____ left.

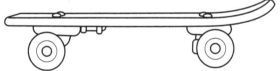

4. 5,648 ÷ 8 =

5. Put the numbers in order from greatest to least.
   79,098   78,008   79,987   78,889

_____

Lesson 159

1. $336 \div 12 =$

2. $789 \div 3 =$

3. $112 \times 471 =$

4. Write the number six million, eight hundred fifty-four thousand, two hundred eight.

   _____

5. The Children's Museum hosted a special exhibit in November and December. A total of 8,762 kids visited the museum during the 2 months it was on display. An equal number of kids visited the exhibit each month. How many students visited the exhibit during November?

   _____ students visited the exhibit during November.

Lesson 160

1. $8,904 \div 24 =$

2. Ms. Simpson is sorting 3,330 books into boxes. She wants to put an equal number of books in each box. She is dividing the books into 15 different boxes. How many books should Ms. Simpson put in each box?

   Ms. Simpson should put _____ books in each box.

3. $901 \times 578 =$

4. $4,893 \div 3 =$

5. Put the numbers in order from least to greatest.
   34,321   33,232   35,453   37,876   371,876

Lesson 161

1. Mimi put $255 in the bank. She earned $7.85 in interest the first year. The second year, Mimi earned twice as much money in interest. How much interest did Mimi earn the second year?

   Mimi earned _____ interest the second year.

2. Round each number to the nearest thousand. Estimate the answer. 45,321 – 43,987 is about _____ .

3. 876 x 897 =

4. 4,338 ÷ 9 =

5. Fill in the blank with <, >, or = to make the number sentence true. 678,987 _____ 675,897

Lesson 162

1. Fill in the blank with <, >, or = to make the number sentence true.
   $\frac{1}{8}$ _____ $\frac{1}{4}$

2. (34 x 67) – 2,098 =

3. 6,584 ÷ 8 =

4. 786,987 – 45,887 =

5. Write the number seven million, six hundred eighty-nine thousand, four hundred one.

_____

Lesson 163

1.   897 x 765 =

2.   448 ÷ 16 =

3.   2,180 ÷ 20 =

4.   The Hat Hut has a selection of 4,578 hats. There are an equal number of cowboy hats, sun hats, and baseball caps for sale. How many baseball caps are for sale at The Hat Hut?

     _____ baseball caps are for sale at The Hat Hut.

5.   Put the numbers in order from least to greatest.
     34,543   34,345   345,456   345,987

Lesson 164

1.   The year is 2004. Maddie was born in 1998. Her grandmother was born in 1938. How old is Maddie? How old is her grandmother? How many years older is Maddie's grandmother than Maddie?

     Maddie is _____. Her grandmother is _____.
     Maddie's grandmother is _____ years older than Maddie.

2.   435 x 786 =

3.   6,576 ÷ 16 =

4.   19n = 133   n = _____

5.   Write the number in standard form.
     7,000,000 + 400,000 + 30,000 + 300 + 7

Lesson 165

1. Circle the even number between 56,800 and 75,000.

   56,789   43,862   66,784   74,545   55,899

2. 64n = 768   n = _____

3. Miriam has saved $212.50. Jeremiah has saved $345.90. Mark has saved 3 times as much money as Miriam. How much money has Mark saved?

   Mark has saved _____.

4. 348,543 – 21,876 =

5. 145 x 876 =

Lesson 166

1. Write the numbers in order from least to greatest.
   233,456   234,454   234,671   203,345   203,479

   _____

2. 5,098 x 75 =

3. 286 ÷ 11 =

4. 768 ÷ 12 =

5. Margaret has 89 quarters in a jar. What is the value of 89 quarters?

   The value of 89 quarters is _____.

Lesson 167

1. $45n = 360$ $n =$ _____

2. $4{,}344 \div 24 =$

3. $878 \times 54 =$

4. Fill in the blank with <, >, or = to make the number sentence true.
   $715{,}550$ _____ $715{,}505$

5. Flora's Flowers has 915 flowers. The florists divide the flowers into bouquets. Each bouquet is made up of 15 flowers. How many bouquets is Flora's Flowers able to make?

   Flora's Flowers is able to make _____ bouquets.

Lesson 168

1. $8{,}108 \times 87 =$

2. Darnell's dad gave him all the dimes from his change jar. Altogether, the dimes make up the value $7.40. How many dimes does Darnell have?

   Darnell has _____ dimes.

3. $208 \times 76 =$

4. $364 \div 13 =$

5. Write the number two million, one hundred ninety-four thousand, six hundred sixteen.

Lesson 169

1. $9,098 \times 34 =$

2. $78n = 1,170$ $n =$ _____

3. $544 \div 16 =$

4. Circle the odd number between 40,000 and 45,000.

   40,700   42,895   45,787   38,284   43,048

5. Cassie has lived in Washington, D.C. for 15 years. There are 365 days in a year and 7 days in a week. How many days has Cassie lived in Washington, D.C.?

   Cassie has lived in Washington, D.C. for _____ days.

Lesson 170

1. Write the numbers in order from greatest to least.
   54,543   55,675   54,009   54,989   540,654

   _____

2. $7,002 \div 18 =$

3. $1,987 \times 17 =$

4. Paige checks the mileage on 3 vehicles. The red station wagon has 123,432 miles on it. The blue van has 213,454 miles on it. The yellow sports car has 233,432 miles on it. How many more miles does the blue van have than the red station wagon?

   The blue van has _____ more miles on it than the red station wagon.

5. $240 \div 4 =$

Lesson 171

1. Fill in the missing numbers to complete the pattern.
212, 224, 248, 260, 284, _____, _____

2. Round each number to the nearest hundred thousands place.
543,456 _____
334,213 _____
213,457 _____
768,789 _____

3. Round each number to the nearest millions place.
23,456,654 _____
1,234,567 _____
4,567,765 _____
45,565,654 _____

4. $90{,}876 - 76{,}789 =$

5. Mrs. Hannon spent 112 quarters buying treats for her class. How much money did Mrs. Hannon spend?

Mrs. Hannon spent _____.

Lesson 172

1. $1{,}312 \div 16 =$

2. $3{,}543 \times 6 =$

3. $843 \times 123 =$

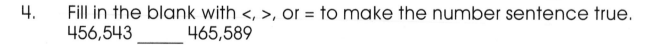

4. Fill in the blank with <, >, or = to make the number sentence true.
456,543 _____ 465,589

5. The mail carrier can deliver 356 letters each hour. How many letters can the mail carrier deliver in 9 hours?

The mail carrier can deliver _____ letters in 9 hours.

Lesson 173

1. 8.87 x 65 =

2. 9.90 x 344 =

3. Macy earned $3.85 raking leaves, $4.50 dusting her house, and $5.25 vacuuming her house. Then, she spent $\frac{1}{2}$ of her money on a new book. How much money does Macy have now?

    Macy has _____ now.

4. 143 x 113 =

5. Fill in the missing letters to complete the pattern.
    Z, Z, A, B, C, W, W, D, E, F, _____, _____, _____

Lesson 174

1. Fill in the missing numbers to complete the pattern.
    2,012, 2,037, 2,062, 2,087, _____, _____

2. 4,671 ÷ 9 =

3. 54,675 – 48,997 =

4. 708 x 456 =

5. If the year is 2005 and Melissa is 34 years old, in what year was Melissa born?

    Melissa was born in the year _____.

Lesson 175

1. 197 x 866 =

2. 644 ÷ 14 =

3. Put the numbers in order from least to greatest.
   676,655   675,565   607,755   675,567

_____

4. 1,998 ÷ 18 =

5. Ms. French bought enough pencils for every student in her school to receive 2 new pencils on the first day of school. There are 1,870 students enrolled in Ms. French's school. How many pencils did Ms. French buy?

   Ms. French bought _____ pencils.

Lesson 176

1. 156 x 203 =

2. 4,345 x 6 =

3. 3,225 ÷ 15 =

4. A baseball league has 200 bags of practice baseballs. There are 189 baseballs in each bag. If $\frac{1}{2}$ of the baseballs are white and the rest of the baseballs are assorted colors, how many baseballs are in all of the bags combined?

   There are _____ baseballs in all of the bags combined.

5. Fill in the missing numbers to complete the pattern.
   3,015, 2,997, 2,979, 2,961, _____, _____

Lesson 177

1. $8,760 \div 12 =$

2. Fill in the blank with <, >, or = to make the number sentence true.
456,347 _____ 356,764

3. $79,004 - 34,789 =$

4. $55n = 440$ $n =$ _____

5. $273 \div 21 =$

Lesson 178

1. Fill in the blank with <, >, or = to make the number sentence true.
298,007 _____ 289,987

2. $8,900 \times 60 =$

3. $65n = 1,170$ $n =$ _____

4. $546 \div 13 =$

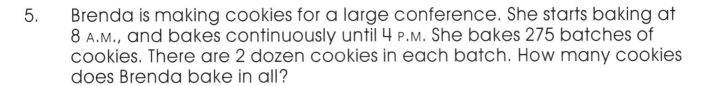

5. Brenda is making cookies for a large conference. She starts baking at 8 A.M., and bakes continuously until 4 P.M. She bakes 275 batches of cookies. There are 2 dozen cookies in each batch. How many cookies does Brenda bake in all?

Brenda bakes _____ cookies in all.

Lesson 179

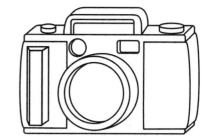

1. $87,908 - 57,678 =$

2. $6,765 \times 8 =$

3. $564 \times 109 =$

4. Janelle works as a photographer for her school's yearbook. At the end of the year, she has a total of 2,448 pictures she wants to divide into 24 equal stacks. How many pictures should Janelle put in each stack?

    Janelle should put _____ photos in each stack.

5. Round the number to the nearest ten thousands place.
   543,765 _____

Lesson 180

1. The library has 266 novels available to be checked out. Each novel is 458 pages long. How many pages are in all 266 novels combined?

    There are _____ pages total in all 266 novels combined.

2. $4,536 \div 21 =$

3. $836 \div 22 =$

4. $720 \div 15 =$

5. First, solve each number sentence. Then, fill in the blank with <, >, or = to make the number sentence true.

    $(4 \times 9 = \underline{\quad})$ _____ $(180 \div 18 = \underline{\quad})$

Answer Key: Lessons 1–19

Lesson 1
1. 649
2. 5,579
3. twenty-first
4. 30,543
5. 100,087

Lesson 2
1. 65,303
2. 6,551
3. 62,884
4. 50,000 + 9,000 + 6
5. $35,528

Lesson 3
1. $90.07
2. 7,444; 7,567; 7,656; 17,456; 71,555
3. 207,632,770
4. $21,980
5. 6,400,002

Lesson 4
1. 50,000
2. 14,438
3. 67,134
4. $11.95
5. 44,000

Lesson 5
1. >
2. 12,600,008
3. 84
4. 372
5. 1,800

Lesson 6
1. 135
2. 608
3. 5
4. 3,000,000 + 400,000 + 90.000 + 6,000 + 700 + 70 + 2
5. 55,678; 54,922; 54,657; 54,607; 45,656

Lesson 7
1. >
2. 729
3. 34
4. $22.12
5. 736

Lesson 8
1. $99.99; $99.90; $99.87; $99.09; $90.87
2. 500,000
3. 21
4. 75
5. 140,000,687

Lesson 9
1. 22,212
2. $76.67; $76.77; $77.06; $77.76; $77.89
3. 9,000,000 + 300,000 + 30,000 + 9,000 + 6
4. 5
5. 9

Lesson 10
1. 8,904,503
2. 216
3. 246
4. 8
5. $13,123.05

Lesson 11
1. 8
2. $1.70
3. 3,065
4. 7,800
5. 6 x 8 = 48

Lesson 12
1. <
2. 41
3. 13
4. 5
5. 11,667

Lesson 13
1. $323
2. >
3. 432
4. 23
5. 6 groups of 7 squares drawn

Lesson 14
1. 578,999
2. =
3. 880
4. 472
5. 440

Lesson 15
1. $13,852
2. 356
3. 536
4. 53
5. 12 x 4 = 48 drawn

Lesson 16
1. 9
2. 632,795
3. 12
4. V; U
5. 8

Lesson 17
1. 1
2. 108
3. 38,908
4. $978.80
5. <

Lesson 18
1. 10
2. 490
3. 10
4. 544
5. 3 x 9 = 27
   9 x 3 = 27

Lesson 19
1. 585
2. 50
3. 27,703
4. 20,442
5. 1,600; 3,200; 12,800

Answer Key: Lessons 20–42

Lesson 20
1. 50
2. 122,631
3. 54
4. $150.00
5.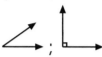

Lesson 21
1. 20
2. 17,000; 1,000; 38,000
3. 129,684
4. 26,665
5. 10,000

Lesson 22
1. 165
2. 31,875
3. 228
4. 639
5. 7,500

Lesson 23
1. 60,000; 120,000; 70,000
2. 120
3. 468
4. 3,456
5. 33

Lesson 24
1. 192
2. 111
3. 14
4. 371
5. Lee; Pierre; Jamestown; Lanier; Martindale

Lesson 25
1. 102
2. 400
3. 10
4. 330
5. 70

Lesson 26
1. 199
2. 100
3. 9
4. 15,000; 2,000; 89,000
5. 192

Lesson 27
1. 60
2. 197,867
3. 369
4. 32,912
5. 154

Lesson 28
1. 16
2. 196
3. 7
4. 177
5. 34

Lesson 29
1. 7,624
2. 12
3. 7
4. 76
5. 18

Lesson 30
1. 9
2. C
3. 22,114
4. 216
5. 116

Lesson 31
1. 4
2. 60
3. 140
4. 126
5. 4,000,769

Lesson 32
1. 32
2. $1.40
3. 32,890
4. 81
5. 3,113

Lesson 33
1. 12
2. A
3. 24
4. 360
5. 121

Lesson 34
1. 7:45
2. 84
3. 75
4. 13,926
5. $2.25

Lesson 35
1. 70,000
2. 176
3. 441
4. 120
5. 110

Lesson 36
1. $1.75
2. 10
3. 9
4. 6
5. 700

Lesson 37
1. $3
2. 21
3. 15
4. 3
5. 16

Lesson 38
1. 162
2. 1,573
3. 15
4. 100
5. 192

Lesson 39
1. 57
2. 11
3. 765
4. 728
5. $462

Lesson 40
1. 472
2. 162
3. 9
4. 568
5. 36

Lesson 41
1. 57
2. 72
3. 600
4. 273
5. 8

Lesson 42
1. 26,253
2. 64; 1,024
3. 204
4. 2,416
5. 84

Answer Key: Lessons 43–61

Lesson 43
1. 744
2. 42
3. 2,008
4. no; answers will vary
5. $\frac{8}{55}$

Lesson 44
1. 85
2. 4,553
3. 287
4. 3,897
5. pentagon, yes; triangle, yes; circle, no; closed figure, yes

Lesson 45
1. square, yes; diamond, yes; pentagon, no; rectangle, yes; answers will vary
2. 126
3. 4,959
4. 24
5. I

Lesson 46
1. 2,337
2. 8,883
3. 18
4. C
5. 163

Lesson 47
1.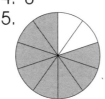
2. 7,021
3. 1,618
4. 8
5.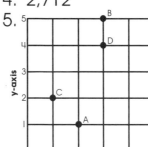

Lesson 48
1. B
2. 19
3. 2,226
4. 3,258
5. $255

Lesson 49
1. 1,000,000
2. 944
3. 539
4. 12
5. $75; $105; $75

Lesson 50
1. 9
2. 80,000 – 30,000 = 50,000
3. 135
4. 6,356
5. $\frac{9}{12}$

Lesson 51
1. 8
2. B
3. 8.4
4. 3,960
5. C

Lesson 52
1. >
2. 12
3. 434
4. 18
5. cylinder

Lesson 53
1. 307
2. 126
3. 702
4. 2,712
5.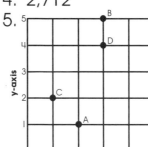

Lesson 54
1. 4.5
2. 49
3. 7,092
4. 70
5. cube

Lesson 55
1. D
2. 100
3. 804.6
4. 44,415
5. >

Lesson 56
1. 24
2. 34,989
3. 40,550
4. $7.50
5. 944

Lesson 57
1. rectangular prism
2. 17,880
3. 76
4. 144
5.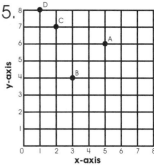

Lesson 58
1. 136.2
2. 52,320
3. 18
4. $1.95
5. 448

Lesson 59
1. <
2. 3,648
3. 135
4. 1
5. (8,2)

Lesson 60
1. 112
2. 3,171
3. 56
4. <
5. 12,489

Lesson 61
1. 980,507
2. 25,980
3. 0.186
4. C
5. 445

Answer Key: Lessons 62–77

Lesson 62
1. 187
2. 30,000
3. 36,280
4. 29
5. 4

Lesson 63
1. 43,546; 43,765; 54,678; 54,897; 55,678
2. 1,872
3. 70,000 + 6,000 + 700 + 80 + 9
4. 1
5. 9:05

Lesson 64
1. A
2. 637
3. 24
4. eighty-nine thousand, nine hundred eighty
5. 258

Lesson 65
1. one hundred three thousand, five hundred sixty-seven
2. 6,570
3. 288
4. 8,136
5. 775,987; 750,654; 750,546; 705,908; 705,098

Lesson 66
1. A
2. 6,960
3. 8
4. 578,601
5. $283.50

Lesson 67
1. C
2. 23,940
3. 29
4. 160
5. 740,303

Lesson 68
1. 679,604
2. 1,332
3. 6,160
4. 15
5. 4

Lesson 69
1. $68.85
2. 55,456; 54,345; 54,343; 43,454
3. 129
4. 47,580
5. 0

Lesson 70
1. 1,728
2. 35
3. 30,618
4. $\frac{1}{8}$; $\frac{1}{4}$; $\frac{4}{8}$; $\frac{2}{3}$
5. 3

Lesson 71
1. 1,724
2. 80,000 − 50,000 = 30,000
3. the last thermometer is circled
4. 30,006
5. 81

Lesson 72
1. 256; 1
2. 32,912
3. 81.9
4. 44,495
5.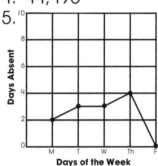

Lesson 73
1. 165
2. 336
3. 10
4. 41,407
5. $5.25

Lesson 74
1. 39,886
2. 19,890
3. 16
4. 44,335
5. 389;

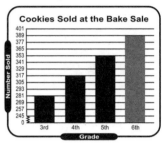

Lesson 75
1. 11,356
2. $8\frac{1}{2}$
3. 8,008
4. 21,912
5. 98

Lesson 76
1. 90
2. 1/27/02
3. 91
4. 41,172
5. 115

Lesson 77
1. 153
2. 19,701
3. 8,492
4. 72
5. 14; 9

Answer Key: Lessons 78–99

Lesson 78
1. 64
2. 27,648
3. 90
4. 42,924
5. $5\frac{1}{2}$

Lesson 79
1. 27
2. 78,210
3. 44,748
4. inch
5. 498

Lesson 80
1. 294
2. 50,381
3. 22,820
4. 501
5. 228 ft.^{2}

Lesson 81
1. cylinder
2. 241,644
3. 192
4. 120.75
5. 12 in.

Lesson 82
1. 2,006
2. 22,542
3. 152,295
4. 100 ft.
5. 625 ft.^{2}

Lesson 83
1. ray
2. segment
3. 21,105
4. 51,781
5. 4,806

Lesson 84
1. 69
2. 12
3. 11,745
4. 18,008
5. 8

Lesson 85
1. 10,490
2. 751.75
3. 2,532.15
4. 15
5. pyramid

Lesson 86
1. $252
2. 104,676
3. 225
4. 70
5. 63 ft.^{2}

Lesson 87
1. 145,530
2. 27,148
3. 12:10
4. 257
5. 18.84

Lesson 88
1. 210
2. 9
3. 10,668
4. 47,394
5. obtuse

Lesson 89
1. 1,130; 2
2. 72.2
3. 48,327
4. 52,056
5. 10; 31.4

Lesson 90
1. 4,368
2. 163.2
3. 3,194.8
4. 22,296
5. 36

Lesson 91
1. 29; 8
2. 6
3. 21,435
4. 17
5. answers will vary

Lesson 92
1. 1,013
2. 109
3. 46,996
4. 6
5. first angle circled

Lesson 93
1. 3,530
2. 2,052
3. 18,333
4. 761
5. rotation

Lesson 94
1. answers will vary
2. 36; 72
3. 11,439
4. Brown
5. Red or Green

Lesson 95
1. 11,900; 23,800
2. first triangle circled
3. 79,716
4. 1,356
5. 1,014

Lesson 96
1. 100
2. 7,987
3. 29,256
4. 87
5. answers will vary

Lesson 97
1. 3,894
2. 10,025
3. 7,008
4. 73,485
5. last star circled

Lesson 98
1. answers will vary
2. 10,881
3. 49
4. 69,420
5. rectangular prism

Lesson 99
1. 5
2. 54,120
3. 9
4. 10,998
5. 4,911

Answer Key: Lessons 100–121

Lesson 100
1. 4:50 P.M.
2. 70,136
3. 363
4. 72
5. answers will vary

Lesson 101
1. 232
2. 91
3. 28,512
4. 2,441
5. 152 in.

Lesson 102
1. 225
2. answers will vary
3. 126
4. 125
5. 9

Lesson 103
1. 295,268
2. 1:15 P.M.
3. 2,673
4. 10,560
5. 2.5 centimeters

Lesson 104
1. 315,225
2. 863
3. 1,307
4. 5
5. 762

Lesson 105
1. $986.25
2. 670,140
3. 96
4. 211
5. meter

Lesson 106
1. 13,979
2. 998
3. 108
4. 10,000
5. 320

Lesson 107
1. $93.50
2. 10 gallons
3. 233,117
4. 2,379
5. pound

Lesson 108
1. 42,295
2. 853
3. 200
4. 60
5. 80° F

Lesson 109
1. $2.55
2. 8
3. 28,083
4. 40
5. B

Lesson 110
1. gallon
2. 1,998
3. 99
4. 51,467
5. 8 in.

Lesson 111
1. 6:35 A.M.
2. 360
3. 30,966
4. 34
5. 18

Lesson 112
1. 14,553
2. >
3. 48
4. 100,956
5. 16

Lesson 113
1. 228
2. 1 gram
3. 346,995
4. 300
5. freezing

Lesson 114
1. 3,948
2. 701
3. 210,192
4. 390,728
5. 126 in.^{2}

Lesson 115
1. 14
2. 206
3. 1,028
4. 4
5. 72

Lesson 116
1. 405
2. 53,010
3. 1,245
4. 23,398
5. 209

Lesson 117
1. 10° C
2. 1,137
3. 1,000
4. 232,875
5. $5\frac{1}{2}$

Lesson 118
1. 403
2. 300
3. 660
4. 166,428
5. 5 inches

Lesson 119
1. 914
2. <
3. 30,616
4. 10
5. 605,475

Lesson 120
1. $43
2. 1,283
3. 10,775
4. 16,750
5. 11:00 P.M.

Lesson 121
1. 28,840
2. $\frac{2}{2}$
3. 66,314
4. 938
5. 59,736

Answer Key: Lessons 122–141

Lesson 122
1. 1,142
2. 187,264
3. 7,800,061
4. 3,765
5. 84,708

Lesson 123
1. 71,323; 70,656; 65,655; 17,987
2. fifty-four thousand, eight hundred seventy-six
3. $109.00
4. 253,164
5. pentagon

Lesson 124
1. 18,009; 18,879; 18,989; 81,234
2. 62,556
3. 33,768
4. $224.23
5. obtuse

Lesson 125
1. 32,678; 98,000
2. $1,229
3. 111
4. 543,120
5. △

Lesson 126
1. 112,878; 111,987; 101,565; 101,543
2. $236.85
3. 392,445
4. 352,889
5. 25

Lesson 127
1. 3,786
2. 45,675; 102,673
3. 743,201
4. 40,629
5. 538

Lesson 128
1. 14
2. 788,463
3. 49,090
4. 281.26
5. 258,608

Lesson 129
1. 129
2. 79,024
3. 507
4. 468,766
5. 55,098; 54,666; 54,456; 51,987

Lesson 130
1. $10
2. 42,612
3. 158
4. 350,007
5. 166,345

Lesson 131
1. 101
2. 14,931
3. 13
4. 515.28
5. $96.00

Lesson 132
1. 264
2. 18
3. 163,812
4. 770.28
5. $0.75

Lesson 133
1. 21
2. 306,765
3. 12,000
4. 49,068
5. 420

Lesson 134
1. 17
2. 14,329
3. 2,064
4. 33
5. $3.75

Lesson 135
1. 49,533
2. 200
3. 55,309
4. 159,744
5. 675

Lesson 136
1. 70
2. 956
3. 480,924
4. 31
5. 60

Lesson 137
1. 168
2. 49,555
3. 27
4. 864,612
5. 352

Lesson 138
1. 714
2. 758.48
3. 39,826.3
4. 475,668
5. June

Lesson 139
1. 5
2. 69.96
3. 47,436
4. 5,610
5. 216

Lesson 140
1. 15
2. 15,069.6
3. 72.96
4. 98
5. 177

Lesson 141
1. 0
2. 480,000
3. 1,134; 3,402
4. 26,724
5. 293; 8

Answer Key: Lessons 142–161

Lesson 142
1. 47,613
2. 10,881
3. 200
4. 11,700
5. 828; 678; 378

Lesson 143
1. 31; 10
2. 20,000
3. 359,784
4. 196
5. X through 234,459; 234,345; 34,677

Lesson 144
1. 19,557
2. 77
3. 1,349; 1,461
4. 41,496
5. 252

Lesson 145
1. 50,000; 30,000; 130,000; 90,000
2. $505.05
3. 106,512
4. 400
5. 269; 250; 231

Lesson 146
1. 300,000; 300,000; 1,000,000; 900,000
2. 4,455
3. 13
4. 132
5. $1.75

Lesson 147
1. 393,711
2. 1,000,000; 3,000,000; 2,000,000
3. 2,128
4. 759; 762; 750
5. 150

Lesson 148
1. 331,525
2. 123
3. 686
4. T; G
5. 40

Lesson 149
1. 3,000; 14,000; 146,000; 5,000
2. 14,528
3. 60
4. 316; 301; 331
5. 30,876

Lesson 150
1. $1,190.00
2. 64,440
3. 12,582
4. 204
5.

Lesson 151
1. 2,291
2. 7,633,014
3. 237,876
4. 28,014
5. 500

Lesson 152
1. 243,320
2. 10,000
3. 5,192
4. five hundred sixty thousand, six hundred fifty-four
5. 11,832

Lesson 153
1. 394.2
2. $103.50
3. 9
4. 348,840
5. 54,323

Lesson 154
1. 807
2. 97,733
3. 652
4. 855
5. 44,565; 45,456; 45,675; 46,567

Lesson 155
1. 21
2. 80,876
3. 26,070
4. 74,556
5. 1,867

Lesson 156
1. 17,192
2. 540
3. 1,975
4. 1,000
5. one hundred forty-four thousand, six hundred fifty-seven

Lesson 157
1. 4,939.5
2. 79,803
3. 15.54
4. 3,718,612
5. 219,312

Lesson 158
1. twelve million, two hundred thirty-four thousand
2. 58,896
3. $663.27
4. 706
5. 79,987; 79,098; 78,889; 78,008

Lesson 159
1. 28
2. 263
3. 52,752
4. 6,854,208
5. 4,381

Lesson 160
1. 371
2. 222
3. 520,778
4. 1,631
5. 33,232; 34,321; 35,453; 37,876; 371,876

Lesson 161
1. $15.70
2. 1,000
3. 785,772
4. 482
5. >

Answer Key: Lessons 162–180

Lesson 162
1. <
2. 180
3. 823
4. 741,100
5. 7,689,401

Lesson 163
1. 686,205
2. 28
3. 109
4. 1,526
5. 34,345; 34,543;
   345,456;
   345,987

Lesson 164
1. 6; 66; 60
2. 341,910
3. 411
4. 7
5. 7,430,307

Lesson 165
1. 66,784
2. 12
3. $637.50
4. 326,667
5. 127,020

Lesson 166
1. 203,345;
   203,479;
   234,454;
   233,456;
   234,671
2. 382,350
3. 26
4. 64
5. $22.25

Lesson 167
1. 8
2. 181
3. 47,412
4. >
5. 61

Lesson 168
1. 705,396
2. 74
3. 15,808
4. 28
5. 2,194,616

Lesson 169
1. 309,332
2. 15
3. 34
4. 42,895
5. 5,475

Lesson 170
1. 540,654;
   55,675; 54,989;
   54,543; 54,009
2. 389
3. 33,779
4. 90,022
5. 60

Lesson 171
1. 296; 320
2. 500,000;
   300,000;
   200,000;
   800,000
3. 23,000,000;
   1,000,000;
   5,000,000;
   46,000,000
4. 14,087
5. $28.00

Lesson 172
1. 82
2. 21,258
3. 103,689
4. <
5. 3,204

Lesson 173
1. 576.55
2. 3,405.6
3. $6.80
4. 16,159
5. T; T; G

Lesson 174
1. 2,112; 2,137
2. 519
3. 5,678
4. 322,848
5. 1971

Lesson 175
1. 170,602
2. 46
3. 607,755;
   675,565;
   675,567;
   676,655
4. 111
5. 3,740

Lesson 176
1. 31,668
2. 26,070
3. 215
4. 37,800
5. 2,943; 2,925

Lesson 177
1. 730
2. >
3. 44,215
4. 8
5. 13

Lesson 178
1. >
2. 534,000
3. 18
4. 42
5. 6,600

Lesson 179
1. 30,230
2. 54,120
3. 61,476
4. 102
5. 540,000

Lesson 180
1. 121,828
2. 216
3. 38
4. 48
5. 36; >; 10

Assessment 1 (Lessons 1–10)

Name _____

1. 97,786 – 94,566 =

   A. 192,352
   B. 3,022
   C. 3,220
   D. 2,022

2. $450.67 + y = $765.67
   y =

   A. $305.05
   B. $315.55
   C. $315.00
   D. $1,216.34

3. Order the numbers from least to greatest.
   56,700; 65,767; 56,005; 55,676; 56,007

   A. 56,005; 56,007; 55,676; 56.700; 65,767
   B. 55,676; 56,005; 56,007; 56,700; 65,767
   C. 56,700; 56,007; 56,005; 55,676; 65,767
   D. 65,676; 56,700; 56,007; 56,005; 55,676

4. What is the number in standard form?
   6,000,000 + 700,000 + 80,000 + 7,000 + 2

   A. 6,787,002
   B. 678,702
   C. 6,787,200
   D. 6,782,702

5. Make the number sentence true.
   75,676 _____ 75,677

   A. >
   B. <
   C. =
   D. 74,564

6. What is the number 17,876,004 in word form?

   A. seventeen million, eight hundred and six thousand, four
   B. seventeen million, eight hundred seventy-six thousand, four hundred
   C. seventeen million, eight hundred seventy-six thousand, four
   D. seven million, eight hundred seventy-six thousand, four

7. Which is the smallest number?

   A. 78,090
   B. 78,900
   C. 87,676
   D. 78,009

8. Brooke has a sticker album with 78 stickers on each page. There are 9 pages in Brooke's sticker album. How many stickers are there on all 9 pages?

   A. 702
   B. 70
   C. 712
   D. 87

Assessment 2 (Lessons 11–20)

Name _____

1. Look at the picture. Circle the 2 number sentences that the picture could possibly represent.

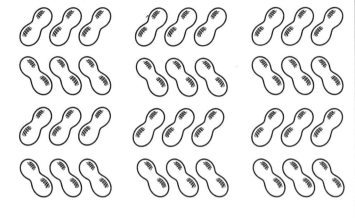

A. 12 x 4; 12 ÷ 3 =
B. 12 x 3; 36 ÷ 3 =
C. 12 x 4; 38 ÷ 4 =
D. 12 + 2; 12 ÷ 3 =

2. Which number is missing from the pattern?
2, 8, 32, _____, 512

A. 64
B. 114
C. 128
D. 121

3. 87,897 + y = 123,786
y =

A. 211,683
B. 38,889
C. 35,809
D. 35,889

4. 67,786 – 44,788 =

A. 23,001
B. 23,110
C. 22,998
D. 112,574

5. Fill in the missing number to complete the pattern.
2,000, 1,825, _____, 1,475, 1,300

A. 1,500
B. 1,650
C. 1,875
D. 2,250

6. Fill in the missing shape to complete the pattern.

A. ◻
B. ◇
C. ◻
D. ◇

7. Stefanie runs 44 miles every week. How many miles does Stefanie run in 6 weeks?

A. 818
B. 51
C. 204
D. 264

8. To help his teacher, Jeremy divides 88 pens into 4 piles. He put an equal number of pens in each pile. How many pens does Jeremy place in each pile?

A. 21
B. 22
C. 18
D. 12

Assessment 3 (Lessons 21–30)

Name _____

1. 6 x 5 =

A. 30
B. 32
C. 35
D. 11

2. 10 x 9 =

A. 90
B. 91
C. 95
D. 109

Use the bar graph for questions 3 and 4.

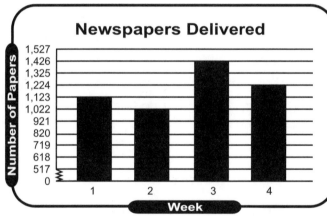

Newspapers Delivered

3. How many more newspapers were delivered in Weeks 3 and 4 than in Weeks 1 and 2?

A. 509
B. 491
C. 500
D. 505

4. How many newspapers were delivered during all of June?

A. 4,975
B. 4,795
C. 4,995
D. 4,575

5. 8 x 8 =

A. 16
B. 64
C. 65
D. 16

6. What is the best estimate for 24,567 + 34,322 = ?

A. 56,500
B. 57,000
C. 59,000
D. 65,000

7. Look at the menu. How many hot dogs can Leigh buy for $10?

A. 7 hot dogs
B. 13 hot dogs
C. 12 hot dogs
D. 6 hot dogs

Greg's Great Food Stand	
Item	**Price**
Soda	$1.25
Hot Dog	$1.00 each or 2 for $1.50
Ice Cream Sandwich	$.75
Hamburger and Fries	$3.25
Lemonade	$.75
Fruit Bowl	$2.75

8. Which number shows 4 millions, 2 hundred thousands, 5 hundreds, and 6 ones?

A. 4,220,506
B. 4,200,560
C. 4,200,506
D. 420,506

Assessment 4 (Lessons 31–40)

Name _____

1. $49 \div 7 =$

A. 10
B. 8
C. 7
D. 14

2. $27 \times 9 =$

A. 44
B. 244
C. 243
D. 203

3. $18 \times 8 =$

A. 104
B. 144
C. 141
D. 152

4. $16,767 - 15,599 =$

A. 1,168
B. 1,167
C. 32,366
D. 1,106

5. Dan drinks 2 cups of juice at breakfast and 2 cups of juice at dinner. How many cups of juice does Dan drink in 7 days?

A. 14
B. 27
C. 28
D. 10

6. Sam recycled 512 cans in May. If he recycled twice as many cans in June, how many cans did he recycle in June?

A. 1,025
B. 1,024
C. 1,014
D. 1,012

Use the pictograph to answer questions 7 and 8.

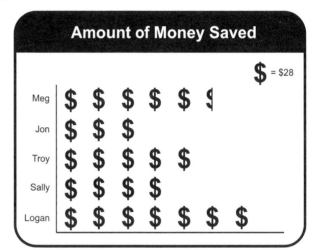

7. How much more money did Meg and Logan save than Jon and Troy?

A. $105
B. $126
C. $155
D. $154

8. Which person was able to save as much money as Jon and Sally combined?

A. Troy
B. Meg
C. Logan
D. Sally

Assessment 5 (Lessons 41–50)   Name _____

1. I am a polygon. I have 5 sides. What shape am I?

   A. triangle
   B. octagon
   C. hexagon
   D. pentagon

2. Round your answer to the nearest thousands place.
   $67,876 - 43,786 =$

   A. 25,000
   B. 24,000
   C. 24,500
   D. 24,900

3. $785 \div 5 =$

   A. 157
   B. 158
   C. 155
   D. 160

4. $59 \times 8 =$

   A. 407
   B. 178
   C. 471
   D. 472

5. How many vertices do 6 rectangles have?

   A. 16
   B. 25
   C. 24
   D. 20

6. Which shape is not a polygon?

   A.
   B.
   C.
   D.

7. Circle the statement below that best describes what is happening in the pattern.
   7, 49, 48, 336, 335, 2,345, 2,344

   A. Each number is being multiplied by 6. Then, 1 is being taken away from each number.
   B. Each number is being multiplied by 6. Then, 1 is being added to each number.
   C. Each number is being multiplied by 7. Then, 1 is being taken away from each number.
   D. Six is being taken away from each number. Then, 5 is being added to each number.

8. Drew is selling old T-shirts at a garage sale. He has 27 boxes of T-shirts to sell. There are 50 T-shirts in each box. The garage sale will last from 7 A.M. to 3 P.M. on Saturday. How many T-shirts is Drew selling in all?

   A. 1,407
   B. 135
   C. 1,350
   D. 1,370

1. Make the number sentence true.
   201,543 _____ 210,767

   A. <
   B. >
   C. =
   D. 209,767

2. Look at the following pattern, or net. If you cut out and folded the net, what 3-dimensional figure would you have?

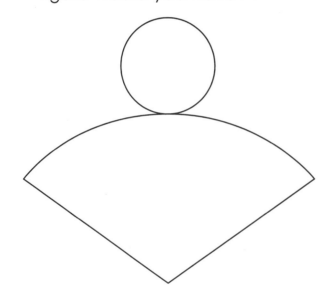

   A. rectangular prism
   B. cube
   C. cone
   D. cylinder

3. What is the value of a pyramid if each triangle = $1.00 and the base = $4.00?

   A. $8.00
   B. $19.00
   C. $9.00
   D. $10.00

4. 978 x 41 =

   A. 40,098
   B. 41,998
   C. 40,998
   D. 40,089

5. 459 x 6 =

   A. 2,074
   B. 2,474
   C. 2,574
   D. 2,754

6. 792 ÷ 9 =

   A. 87
   B. 88
   C. 89
   D. 98

7. 497 ÷ 7 =

   A. 70
   B. 71
   C. 72
   D. 73

8. Olivia has 128 pieces of candy in a bag. If $\frac{3}{4}$ of the pieces are chewing gum and the rest of the pieces are chocolate, how many pieces of chocolate does Olivia have in the bag?

   A. 32
   B. 95
   C. 96
   D. 31

1. 712 x 34 =

A. 24,208
B. 24,280
C. 24,288
D. 24,880

2. Which is the number five hundred eighty-seven thousand, six hundred three?

A. 507,603
B. 587,603
C. 587,630
D. 507,630

3. What is the expanded form of the number 210,234?

A. 20,000 + 1,000 + 200 + 30 + 4
B. 200,000 + 1,000 + 200 + 30 + 4
C. 200,000 + 10,000 + 200 + 30 + 4
D. 200,000 + 10,000 + 30 + 4

4. How many lines of symmetry does the flower have?

A. 4
B. 5
C. 2
D. 0

5. What motion was used to get from the first figure to the second figure?

A. slide
B. flip
C. turn
D. left

6. Put the following numbers in order from least to greatest.
345,543 234,456 787,567
343,565 234,506

A. 234,506; 234,456; 343,565; 345,543; 787,567
B. 787,567; 345,543; 343,565; 234,506; 234,456
C. 234,456; 343,565; 234,506; 345,543; 787,567
D. 234,456; 234,506; 343,565; 345,543; 787,567

7. 896 x 67 =

A. 6,340
B. 60,320
C. 60,332
D. 60,032

8. 150 ÷ 15 =

A. 9
B. 12
C. 1
D. 10

1. Determine the volume of the rectangular prism.

   A. 81 cubic units
   B. 18 cubic units
   C. 80 cubic units
   D. 64 cubic units

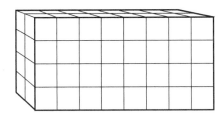

2. Determine the area of the rectangle.

   A. 218 in.²
   B. 280 in.²
   C. 288 in.²
   D. 208 in.²

12 in.

24 in.

3. Kelsey wants to build a fence around her property. What is the perimeter of Kelsey's property?

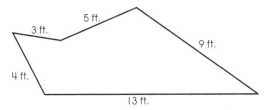

5 ft.
3 ft.
9 ft.
4 ft.
13 ft.

   A. 41 feet
   B. 34 feet
   C. 32 feet
   D. 35 feet

4. 6,765 x 7 =

   A. 47,345
   B. 47,305
   C. 47,533
   D. 47,355

5. Look at the line graph. Which year had the highest gas prices?

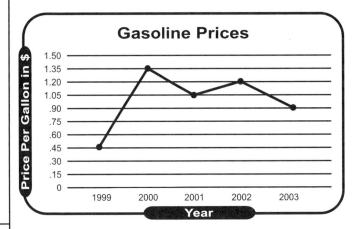

Gasoline Prices

Price Per Gallon in $

1.50 1.35 1.20 1.05 .90 .75 .60 .45 .30 .15 0

1999 2000 2001 2002 2003

Year

   A. 2000
   B. 2001
   C. 1999
   D. 2002

6. 567 ÷ 9 =

   A. 64
   B. 62
   C. 69
   D. 63

7. (916 x 78) – 14 =

   A. 74,405
   B. 71,404
   C. 71,435
   D. 71,434

8. If 1,500 people sign up to run a race, and half of the people who sign up are girls, how many girls sign up to run the race?

   A. 1,000
   B. 1,500
   C. 500
   D. 750

Assessment 9 (Lessons 81–90)　　Name _____

1. What is the best estimate of the circumference of the circle?

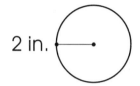

2 in.

A. 12 inches
B. 4 inches
C. 6 inches
D. 18 inches

2. What is the perimeter of the shape below?

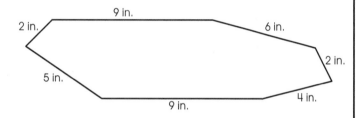

9 in.
2 in.
6 in.
2 in.
5 in.
9 in.
4 in.

A. 42 inches
B. 40 inches
C. 41 inches
D. 37 inches

3. I am a 3-dimensional shape. All of my faces are the same shape. What shape am I?

A. a square pyramid
B. a rectangular prism
C. a sphere
D. a cube

4. 786 x 54 =

A. 40,344
B. 40,444
C. 42,443
D. 42,444

5. Which word best describes the angle below?

A. acute
B. obtuse
C. right
D. left

6. Which name best describes the figure below?

E　　　　　　　　　　　　　F

A. line EF
B. line segment EF
C. ray EF
D. parallel lines EF

7. 8,878 x 89 =

A. 790,144
B. 79,142
C. 790,142
D. 791,142

8. 765 ÷ 15 =

A. 57
B. 52
C. 51
D. 50

Assessment 10 (Lessons 91–100)

Name _____

1. Which flower does not have a line of symmetry?

A.

B.

C.

D.

2. Which statement below best describes a sphere?

A. I have 3 vertices.
B. I am a 2-dimensional shape.
C. My shape consists of 3 circles.
D. My entire surface is curved.

3. Which of the words below best describes the shape of a trash can?

A. cone
B. cylinder
C. sphere
D. square

4. 76,972 – 59,189 =

A. 17,783
B. 17,789
C. 17,873
D. 136,161

5. There are 365 days in a year. There are 52 weeks in a year. Which of the following number sentences would you use to determine the number of days in a week?

A. 365 divided by 7 =
B. 365 x 5 =
C. 365 – 5 =
D. 365 divided by 52 =

6. (78 x 61) divided by 6 =

A. 793
B. 794
C. 795
D. 4,758

7. 1,098 x 5 =

A. 5,440
B. 5,490
C. 222
D. 5,404

8. There are 800 frogs hopping around in a lake. The lake has 40 lily pads. There are an equal number of frogs on each lily pad. How many frogs are on each lily pad?

A. 20
B. 22
C. 28
D. 40

Assessment 11 (Lessons 101–110)   Name _____

1. (86 x 50) ÷ 4 =

    A. 1,157
    B. 1,075
    C. 1,371
    D. 1,177

2. 24 feet = _____ yards

    A. 6
    B. 8
    C. 12
    D. 9

3. Which of the following units of measure would be best to describe the weight of a pencil?

    A. yards
    B. pounds
    C. ounces
    D. inches

4. What temperature is shown on the thermometer?

    A. 95° F
    B. 18° F
    C. 90° F
    D. 91° F

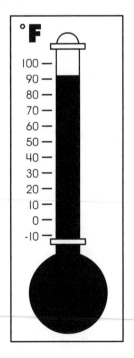

5. 2 tons = _____ pounds

    A. 4,000
    B. 2,000
    C. 5,000
    D. 1,000

6. (765 x 65) – 7,098 =

    A. 42,624
    B. 42,627
    C. 42,634
    D. 42,667

7. 8,184 ÷ 6 =

    A. 1,264
    B. 1,364
    C. 49,104
    D. 49,114

8. Kendra's softball game ended 2 hours and 35 minutes before she went to bed. Kendra went to bed at 9:15 P.M. What time did Kendra's softball game end?

    A. 7:10 A.M.
    B. 6:25 P.M.
    C. 7:40 P.M.
    D. 6:40 P.M.

Assessment 12 (Lessons 111–120)   Name _____

1. Find the volume of the rectangular prism.

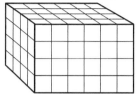

A. 86 cubic units
B. 94 cubic units
C. 96 cubic units
D. 90 cubic units

2. Bethany left the dentist's office at 4:20 P.M. Her appointment lasted for 1 hour and 55 minutes. At what time did Bethany's dentist appointment begin?

A. 2:25 P.M.
B. 2:20 P.M.
C. 2:50 P.M.
D. 3:25 P.M.

3. What is the length of the leaf?

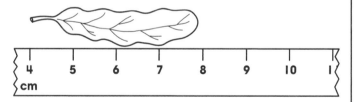

A. 4 centimeters
B. 4 inches
C. 8 centimeters
D. 5 centimeters

4. 4 gallons = _____ quarts

A. 16
B. 14
C. 12
D. 8

5. 0.85 x 6 =

A. 51
B. 5.5
C. 0.51
D. 5.1

6. Determine the area of the triangle.

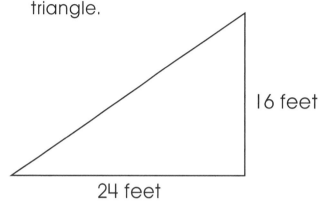

A. 129 ft.^{2}
B. 190 ft.^{2}
C. 192 ft.^{2}
D. 194 ft.^{2}

7. Tamika earned $5.65 per day for 4 days in a row. How much did Tamika earn in all?

A. $22.60
B. $25.65
C. $22.65
D. $20.75

8. 543 x 79 =

A. 42,987
B. 42,897
C. 40,987
D. 41,678

1. What is the volume of the rectangular prism?

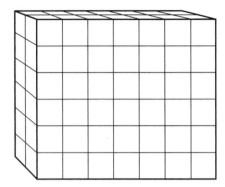

A. 18 cubic units
B. 86 cubic units
C. 85 cubic units
D. 84 cubic units

2. Circle the number one million, six hundred ninety-seven thousand, fourteen.

A. 1,698,140
B. 1,697,014
C. 1,679,014
D. 167,914

3. Put the numbers in order from least to greatest.
799,987; 709,987; 798,098; 709,089

A. 799,987; 799,098; 709,987; 709,089
B. 709,089; 709,987; 799,987; 799,098
C. 709,089; 709,987; 798,098; 799,987
D. 709,987; 709,089; 799,098; 799,987

4. How many vertices do 6 rectangular prisms have?

A. 12
B. 42
C. 45
D. 48

5. What is the area of the triangle?

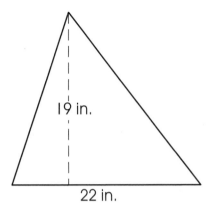

19 in.
22 in.

A. 209 in.^{2}
B. 219 in.^{2}
C. 412 in.^{2}
D. 418 in.^{2}

6. Which written form represents the number 67,987?

A. six hundred thousand, nine hundred eighty-seven
B. sixty-seven thousand, nine hundred eighty-seven
C. sixty-seven, nine hundred eighty-seven
D. sixty-seven hundred, nine hundred eighty-seven

7. $7,896 \div 14 =$

A. 566
B. 644
C. 546
D. 564

8. $(345 \times 78) - 8,006 =$

A. 18,094
B. 18,940
C. 18,904
D. 81,904

Assessment 14 (Lessons 131–140)

Name _____

1. 546 x 234 =

A. 127,765
B.   12,764
C. 127,764
D. 126,765

2. 589 x 876 =

A.   51,864
B. 515,964
C. 515,694
D.   51,586

Use the bar graph below to answer questions 3 and 4.

3. During Week 5, twice as much money was earned as during Weeks 1 and 3. How much money was earned during Week 5?

A. $555
B. $1,012
C. $1,011
D. $1,210

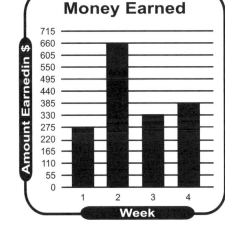

Money Earned

Amount Earned in $

715
660
605
550
495
440
385
330
275
220
165
110
55
0

1   2   3   4
Week

4. How much more money was earned during Weeks 2 and 4 than Weeks 1 and 3?

A. $410
B. $425
C. $440
D. $445

5. 597 ÷ 3 =

A. 198
B. 197
C. 199
D. 196

Use the pictograph below to answer questions 6 and 7.

6. How many more computers were purchased for McNeese and Jefferson than MacArthur and Beaumont?

A. 500
B. 575
C. 400
D. 375

7. How many computers were purchased for all 4 schools combined?

A. 1,550
B. 1,750
C. 1,525
D. 1,765

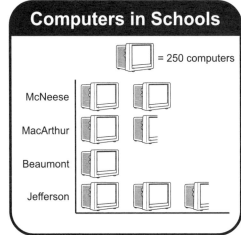

Computers in Schools

= 250 computers

McNeese

MacArthur

Beaumont

Jefferson

8. 99.9 x 103 =

A. 102.897
B. 10,289.7
C. 102,897.0
D. 112,345.7

1. Fill in the missing letters to complete the pattern.
   C, C, F, G, G, J, K, K, ___, ___, ___

   A. O, P, P
   B. N, O, O
   C. N, N, O
   D. K, L, M

2. Fill in the missing numbers to complete the pattern.
   24, 48, 96, 192, ___, ___

   A. 384; 768
   B. 384; 765
   C. 385; 767
   D. 769; 344

3. Fill in the missing numbers to complete the pattern.
   803, 794, 813, 804, 823, ___, ___

   A. 841, 797
   B. 801, 798
   C. 815, 835
   D. 814, 833

4. Round the number to the nearest hundred thousands place.
   344,500

   A. 355,000
   B. 350,000
   C. 400,000
   D. 300,000

5. Round the number to the nearest millions place.
   4,985,677

   A. 4,900,000
   B. 4,500,000
   C. 4,000,000
   D. 5,000,000

6. $567 \times 897 =$

   A. 508,599
   B. 509,899
   C. 87,987
   D. 504,879

7. Larry earned $546 last summer and saved it. This summer, he earned twice as much as last summer. If Larry buys a new bike for $128.75, how much money will he have left?

   A. $1,559.50
   B. $1,449.95
   C. $1,509.25
   D. $706.92

8. $294 \div 14 =$

   A. 21
   B. 18
   C. 20
   D. 19

Assessment 16 (Lessons 151–160) Name _____

1. Isabelle is sorting through file folders. She has 548 file folders. There are an equal number of red, green, blue, and yellow file folders. How many yellow file folders does Isabelle have?

   A. 147
   B. 135
   C. 136
   D. 137

2. 437 x 345 =

   A. 105,675
   B. 155,775
   C. 15,765
   D. 150,765

3. 5,040 ÷ 18 =

   A. 280
   B. 284
   C. 28
   D. 288

4. 675 x 54 =

   A. 36,440
   B. 34,650
   C. 36,450
   D. 36,005

5. A large jar of candy is being auctioned off at the school carnival. There are 4,432 pieces of candy in the jar. If $\frac{3}{4}$ of the candies are jellybeans, how many pieces of the candy in the jar are not jelly beans?

   A. 1,108
   B. 3,324
   C. 1,112
   D. 3,334

6. Which is the number eight hundred ninety-five thousand, five hundred fifty?

   A. 895,555
   B. 895,505
   C. 895,550
   D. 89,555

7. Which odd number has the greatest value?

   A. 543,339
   B. 541,909
   C. 504,543
   D. 543,309

8. Which shows a set of even numbers?

   A. 43,342; 45,654; 78,678; 901
   B. 546,232; 45,456; 3,093; 213
   C. 42,546; 54,555; 6,878; 32,123
   D. 43,342; 34,456; 5,450; 21,344

1. $288n = 2{,}016$

   $n =$

   A. 7
   B. 8
   C. 4
   D. 9

2. Mary Beth keeps 94 nickels in her glove compartment. What is the value of all 94 nickels?

   A. $4.70
   B. $4.75
   C. $4.07
   D. $14.40

3. $552 \div 12 =$

   A. 45
   B. 48
   C. 44
   D. 46

4. $4{,}565 \times 9 =$

   A. 41,087
   B. 14,085
   C. 41,085
   D. 4,185

5. $9{,}000 \div 90 =$

   A. 15
   B. 1
   C. 10
   D. 100

6. Which is the number in standard form?
   $4{,}000{,}000 + 300{,}000 + 30{,}000 + 5{,}000 + 8$

   A. 4,435,808
   B. 435,800
   C. 4,335,800
   D. 4,335,008

7. Which answer shows the number seven million, eight hundred eighty-six thousand?

   A. 7,880,606
   B. 7,880,600
   C. 786,000
   D. 7,886,000

8. Nicole multiplied 654 by 6. Next, she divided the answer by 2. What number did Nicole have then?

   A. 1,962
   B. 1,964
   C. 1,269
   D. 3,924

Assessment 18 (Lessons 171–180)   Name _____

1. Solve each number sentence. Then, use <, >, or = to make the number sentence true.
   (809 – 697 = ___) ___ (444 – 109 = ___)

   A. >
   B. <
   C. =
   D. 65

2. Use <, >, or = to make the number sentence true.
   456,567 _____ 456,067

   A. >
   B. <
   C. =
   D. 455,897

3. Put the numbers in order from least to greatest: 54,434; 54,565; 55,006; 54,678

   A. 55,006; 54,565; 54,678; 54,434
   B. 54,434; 54,678; 54,565; 55,006
   C. 54,434; 54,565; 54,678; 55,006
   D. 55,006; 54,434; 54,678; 54,565

4. Fill in the missing numbers to complete the pattern.
   1,011; 1,048; 1,085; 1,122; ___ ; ___

   A. 1,676;   987
   B. 1,049; 1,156
   C. 1,149; 1,186
   D. 1,159; 1,196

5. $5,424 \div 16 =$

   A. 339
   B. 338
   C. 340
   D. 309

6. $242 \div 22 =$

   A. 15
   B. 12
   C. 11
   D. 13

7. $3,104 \div 8 =$

   A. 387
   B. 388
   C. 389
   D. 391

8. $4,676 \div 28 =$

   A. 166
   B. 167
   C. 168
   D. 165

Assessment Answer Keys

Assessment 1
1. C
2. C
3. B
4. A
5. B
6. C
7. D
8. A

Assessment 2
1. B
2. C
3. D
4. C
5. B
6. B
7. D
8. B

Assessment 3
1. A
2. A
3. D
4. B
5. B
6. C
7. B
8. C

Assessment 4
1. C
2. C
3. B
4. A
5. C
6. B
7. B
8. C

Assessment 5
1. D
2. B
3. A
4. D
5. C
6. A
7. C
8. C

Assessment 6
1. A
2. C
3. A
4. A
5. D
6. B
7. B
8. A

Assessment 7
1. A
2. B
3. C
4. A
5. B
6. D
7. D
8. D

Assessment 8
1. D
2. C
3. B
4. D
5. A
6. D
7. D
8. D

Assessment 9
1. A
2. D
3. D
4. D
5. A
6. B
7. C
8. C

Assessment 10
1. D
2. D
3. B
4. A
5. D
6. A
7. B
8. A

Assessment 11
1. B
2. B
3. C
4. D
5. A
6. B
7. B
8. D

Assessment 12
1. C
2. A
3. A
4. A
5. D
6. C
7. A
8. B

Assessment 13
1. D
2. B
3. C
4. D
5. A
6. B
7. D
8. C

Assessment 14
1. C
2. B
3. D
4. C
5. C
6. A
7. B
8. B

Assessment 15
1. B
2. A
3. D
4. D
5. D
6. A
7. C
8. A

Assessment 16
1. D
2. D
3. A
4. C
5. A
6. C
7. A
8. D

Assessment 17
1. A
2. A
3. D
4. C
5. D
6. D
7. D
8. A

Assessment 18
1. B
2. A
3. C
4. D
5. A
6. C
7. B
8. B

Real World Application 1

Record your start and stop times for different activities during a typical school day. Figure out how much time you spend on each activity and record your results below. Share your findings with your classmates.

Today is _____.

Category	Start	Stop	Start	Stop	Start	Stop	Total
Family							
School							
Homework							
Playing							
Sleeping							
Other _____							

Real World Application 2

Find a favorite recipe in a cookbook. List the ingredients below. Estimate the price of each ingredient and your total cost. Then, go to a store and write down the actual price of each ingredient. Compare your estimated and actual totals with your classmates.

Ingredient	Estimated Cost	Actual Cost
1. _____	_____	_____
2. _____	_____	_____
3. _____	_____	_____
4. _____	_____	_____
5. _____	_____	_____
6. _____	_____	_____
7. _____	_____	_____
8. _____	_____	_____
9. _____	_____	_____
Total Cost	_____	_____

Real World Application 3

Estimate the number of students in your grade and the number of students in your entire school. Check with your school secretary or principal to determine how your estimates compare with the actual numbers of students in your grade and school. Find the difference between your estimates and the actual numbers.

Number of Students	Estimated	Actual
In My Grade		
In My School		
Difference		

Real World Application 4

Draw and cut out several of your favorite geometric shapes. Create a picture in the space below. Write the names of three of the shapes on the lines provided. _____

_____

Real World Application 5

Determine and record the distances between your classroom and the locations listed below. Record your results in the table.

Distance from My Classroom

Location	Distance
Media Center	
Cafeteria	
Office	
Playground	
Restroom	

Real World Application 6

Go on a timed pattern hunt! See how many patterns you can find around your school or outdoors in 15 minutes. For example, look at bricks in sidewalks, or windows in buildings. List the patterns and their locations below. Use another sheet of paper if needed.

Pattern Description	Location
1. _____	_____
2. _____	_____
3. _____	_____
4. _____	_____
5. _____	_____
6. _____	_____
7. _____	_____

Real World Application 7

Clip some coupons from your local newspaper. Write several money word problems to go along with the coupons you clipped.

_____

_____

_____

_____

_____

_____

_____

Real World Application 8

Survey your class to find the number of siblings each person has. Create a Venn diagram displaying this information. Then, write a sentence or two explaining your Venn diagram.

_____

_____

_____

_____

Real World Application 9

Two friends each have 63 cents, but they have different combinations of coins. In the space provided, write down all of the possible coin combinations totaling 63 cents.

Real World Application 10

Record the high and low temperatures for 10 school days. Find the average high and low temperatures for that 10-day period.

High and Low Temperatures Over Ten-Day Period

Day	High Temp.	Low Temp.	Day	High Temp.	Low Temp.

Average High: _____   **Average Low:** _____

Real World Application 11

Survey your classmates to find out everyone's favorite days of the week. In the space below, create a picture and bar graph, each showing this information. Compare your graphs with your classmates.

Real World Application 12

Make up an original word problem involving fractions and write it on the lines provided. Write the answer to the problem in the box below. Have a classmate try to solve your word problem.

_____

_____

_____

_____

_____

_____